PALEO DIET: LOSE WEIGHT & EAT WELL

Achieve The Body You've Always Wanted Eating Healthier and More Delicious Than Ever. Includes Recipes That Will Make You Never Want Junk Food Again

Table of Contents

Chapter 1: What is the Paleo Diet? 5

Chapter 2: The Paleo Diet and a Healthier You 17

   The Health Benefits of Paleo 21

Chapter 3: Benefits of a Paleo Diet 30

Chapter 4: Potential Disadvantages of the Paleo Diet 53

Chapter 5: Your First Seven Days on the Paleo Diet 61

   Paleo-Friendly Recipes 75

      Bacon Sweet Potato Skillet 75

      Instant Pot Breakfast Casserole 77

      Sweet Potato Bowl 79

      Grain-Free Veggie Wraps 80

      Sweet Potato Nachos 82

      Chipotle Chicken Salad 83

      Chicken Nuggets 84

      Instant Pot Chili 86

      Instant Pot Tomato Soup 88

Chapter 6: Sometimes You May Want to Indulge 90

   More About Alcohol 92

   The All-Important Coffee 94

   Chocolate to the Rescue 95

   What About Dairy and Red Meat? 96

Conclusion 97

Chapter 1: What is the Paleo Diet?

There is no doubt that most people have heard of the Paleo diet, even if they have no idea what it is. Put simply, the Paleo diet, short for Paleolithic, is a lifestyle inspired by what our ancestors ate ten-thousand years ago. Sometimes, this may even be referred to as the Caveman or the Stone Age diet.

When on this diet people choose to eat foods that our ancestors during the pre-industrial Paleolithic period would eat, and avoid all else. This means that on the Paleo diet people avoid junk food, grains, legumes, dairy, and sugar because our ancestors of that time did not have access to these foods.

Instead, you can enjoy a healthy diet full of flavorful whole and unprocessed foods. These ingredients include meat, shellfish, fish, poultry, eggs, vegetables, roots, fruits, and berries.

But why eat this way? There is some evidence that suggests that our bodies may be predisposed to this way of eating. In fact, the Paleo diet has been shown to lower the risk of common diseases such as diabetes, cancer, and heart disease. It can also help with more everyday problems such as aiding in sustained weight loss, improving sleep, decreasing bloating and gas, improving mood and mental clarity, increasing sustained energy levels, and keeping both the hair and skin healthy.

Many of these effects can be contributed to the many vitamins, minerals, and other nutrients obtained in a diet high in vegetables, fruits, and meat. The elimination of junk foods that contain sugar, high fructose corn syrup, dyes, preservatives, and other unneeded harmful ingredients can also help lead to more balanced blood sugar, weight loss, and the prevention of disease.

Before we begin the science of why the Paleo diet works and the reasons to choose it, it is important to understand that it is not truly a "diet." Rather, Paleo is a healthy lifestyle. It is not a fad diet, a quick weight loss scheme, or a crash diet. You won't lose twenty pounds within your first two weeks only to gain twenty-five pounds back soon after, which is common with crash dieting. Just as veganism is a lifestyle, so too is Paleo. Some people may choose to only follow the Paleo plan temporarily when they feel the need to lose weight and improve their health. Whereas, many people can happily live their entire lives eating this way.

The choice to go Paleo can help you lose weight and maintain weight loss, but the real benefits are those to your health. For this reason, some people choose to go a completely pure Paleo route. They do this by eliminating as many chemicals out of their lifestyle as possible. This even includes switching to natural toothpaste and deodorant. If your budget allows, you can also choose organic and grass-fed options for your foods. Although, while removing these chemicals can be good for your health, it is by no means required to be Paleo.

While the Paleo lifestyle typically recommends avoiding non-Paleolithic foods, some people may find that after adjusting to the standard lifestyle that they can incorporate small amounts of these foods into their diets. For instance, people may choose to indulge in dairy, chocolate, or alcohol on occasion.

However, if you choose to try adding in non-Paleolithic foods, it is recommended that you only do so after having been on the pure Paleo diet for a month. This is because you might find that you have sensitivities to these foods that you are unable to recognize before. By taking these foods out of your diet for a time, and allowing your body a chance to heal, you can better recognize any adverse effects.

You may know the foods to avoid on the Paleo diet, but why exactly avoid them? Don't worry, but the end of this book you will understand all the ins and outs of this lifestyle, its many benefits, and how to customize it for success. But first, let us examine the foods that are now a part of daily life for many people, despite not being eaten during the Paleolithic period.

Gluten

Many people suffer daily from mysterious undiagnosed disease and symptoms, with no idea as to what is causing their problems. Elements of our diets often cause these symptoms, including gluten. This is a protein found in certain grains, most famously wheat, and may disrupt our health.

This is especially prevalent in people who have Celiac disease which causes many symptoms including malnutrition, stomach pains, bloating, fatigue, anemia, and even reproductive difficulties. This is all because when people with Celiac disease, an autoimmune condition, their immune system will attack their own digestive tract.

But people with this disease are not the only ones negatively affected by gluten. These people may not react as negatively as those with Celiac disease, but people with a gluten intolerance can develop a native immune response to gluten. It is estimated that eighteen million Americans suffer from gluten intolerance, but it is difficult to know the exact numbers. This is because the symptoms such as migraines, fatigue, cognitive decline, stomach pains, weight gain or loss, and more, go hand in hand with many types of disease. Due to this, gluten intolerance can be difficult to diagnose.

Grains

There is much wrong with the American recommended food pyramid. Part of the problem is that this pyramid recommends six to eleven servings of grain every day. The problem with this is that simple carbohydrates, such as grains, quickly break down into sugar once digested. This causes a stark increase in blood sugar and insulin.

Consuming such a large amount of grains in a day will only increase your risk of developing insulin resistance. It's easy to see why America is overrun with obesity, diabetes, insulin resistance, and more.

Lectins

This anti-nutrient is found abundantly in raw grains and legumes and is still found in their cooked state, as well. Lectins are found in these plants in order to form a defense against pests, insects, and microorganisms. They can even remain intact through the digestive tract so that the seeds can later on grow!

Because of this, humans are unable to digest lectins. We develop antibodies to protect against them, but this can cause a variety of symptoms and even make a food intolerable to eat. A good example of this is red kidney beans. You never see these sprouted, because when red kidney beans contain an especially harmful lectin. This can cause symptoms in people if they consume as few as four raw and soaked kidney beans.

Dairy

An estimated seventy-five percent of the worldwide population is unable to digest dairy due to an intolerance to casein or lactose. This can include symptoms of bloating, gas, stomach pains, diarrhea, and even more serious conditions such as irritable bowel syndrome.

While many people may believe that dairy is important for bone health, there is no evidence to support this. In fact, one study even found that people who regularly consumed dairy were fifty times more likely to experience bone fractures! This is further proven when you look at countries that traditionally have low dairy intakes. Despite eating such a small amount of dairy, these countries have much lower rates of osteoporosis than America.

Instead of getting your calcium from dairy, you can easily get it from plant-based sources such as kale, broccoli, and oranges. You can even find a decent serving of calcium within salmon!

Legumes

Legumes are most often beans, but they also include peas, alfalfa, lentils, chickpeas, soybeans, carob, tamarind, and peanuts. This is because legumes are simply seeds that grow within a pod, just like all of these ingredients do. While beans and other legumes are not a junk food and may provide some benefits, you can get the same benefits without the drawbacks that come with legumes from other foods. Just as grains contain harmful lectins, so do legumes.

But beans also contain phytoestrogens. These are compounds that can interact in the body the same way as estrogen, the female hormone. The phytoestrogens can bind to your cell receptors causing an overproduction of estrogen and negatively impact the hormonal balance of both women and men.

Refined Sugars

These sugars are any that have been refined or enhanced, this includes sugar cane, corn syrup, rice syrup, date sugar, dextrose, fructose, glucose, sucrose, and much more. These sugars are one of the most addictive forms of processed foods and can affect a person like a drug. Even if a person isn't hungry or doesn't particularly enjoy a specific dish, they can find themselves reaching for more, because of the sugar addiction.

If this wasn't harmful enough, this sugar is known to cause many conditions, especially obesity and diabetes, which are running rampant in modern society. Studies have also shown that refined sugars can lead to an increased risk of cancer.

Processed Foods

Packaged and processed foods are all the rage and for good reason. In the busy lives that exist in our modern society, it is easier to get these foods when we are constantly on the go. These foods can also be addicting when you grow up eating them, and there are cheap options that are easier for people in poverty to afford.

But these processed foods have a big drawback, and that is the way they affect our health. Between the harmful chemicals, preservatives, artificial ingredients, sugar, food coloring, unhealthy fats, and high sodium content these foods offer little to no nutrition.

Instead, eating these foods has been shown to increase disease and obesity. A diet high in processed foods can cause liver damage, anxiety, depression, autoimmune disorders, inflammation, diabetes, heart disease, high cholesterol, cancer, and much more.

The rates of disease have continued to climb, yet by returning to our natural way of eating that our genetics predispose us to, we may be able to greatly reduce the risk of disease. Many people have even found that after beginning the Paleo diet their diseases or illnesses were cured or went into a state of remission. The statistics and studies are staggering. There is a reason why doctors now frequently recommend this lifestyle to their patients.

You should always discuss major dietary changes with your physician, especially if you have a disease or are predisposed to an illness. Although, there is one doctor that is famous for being an expert on the Paleo lifestyle. In fact, Dr. Loren Cordain has studied the lifestyle for over twenty years. He has published much on its nutritional benefits during that time and has given lectures worldwide. Dr. Cordain lives in Colorado, where he is the Professor Emeritus of the Department of Health and Exercise Science at Colorado State University.

Dr. Cordain explains how the over-consumption of sugar in modern society is killing us. Not only that, but it is highly addictive and added in large quantities to most processed foods. Even savory foods frequently add a significant amount of sugar. The United States Department of Agriculture has even reported that each American consumes an average of one hundred and fifty to seventy pounds of sugar every year.

Because of this, Dr. Cordain explains sugar as being similar to a canary that miners would carry into coal mines to watch for danger. This is because sugar is a precursor to many diseases and conditions, including Alzheimer's, cancer, diabetes, obesity, and much more. This is to such a degree that almost every disease has some degree of correlation with an over-consumption of sugar.

As evidence for the addiction that sugar causes, Dr. Cordain cites studies showing its effects on the brain. The hypothalamus portion of our brain is important for maintaining a balanced intake and regulation of food. This section of the brain has been shown to be activated in people who are obese, whereas it isn't in those who are at a leaner weight. This raises concern about the way sugar affects us and the resulting obesity it has been shown to cause.

Despite there being much clear evidence to the addictiveness of sugar, it is a highly political issue. If the effects of sugar were commonly taught, then many conglomerates of processed food would lose profit. These companies rely on sugar to make people eat their food, which is otherwise lacking in many flavors. Which means that if a large portion of the country adopted the Paleolithic lifestyle they would go out of business. The effect of this can be clearly seen when reading the award-winning book by Michael Moss, Salt Sugar Fat: How the Food Giants Hooked Us. It was even revealed that the executives who run the largest processed food companies were previously the executives in the tobacco industry. Yet, these very same people are allowed to influence decisions about whether or not America establishes a recommended daily value percentage for sugar.

Thankfully, we can look elsewhere for this information. The World Health Organization has established a recommended intake of sugar, which is twenty-five grams daily. Although, due to politics they were pushed to state that up to fifty grams a day would be an improvement over what people are currently consuming.

Dr. Cordain has also discussed the effects of the Paleolithic diet on mood disorders, mental illness, inflammatory illnesses, and more. He fully asserts that the Paleo diet has the ability to prevent and even reverse many chronic degenerative diseases.

While there are no current studies showing the effects of the Paleolithic lifestyle on mood disorders, there is other encouraging evidence. For instance, one Belgian study found that by removing gluten and dairy from the diet people were able to greatly improve in both fatigue levels and mood. Since the Paleo diet already requires the removal of these two ingredients and more, it is hypothesized that it would have an even more beneficial effect.

Studies have shown that one of the major underlying causes of depression, anxiety, and other mood disorders is chronic inflammation. This is because the inflammation impacts our neurotransmitters, neural plasticity, and more. But the Paleo diet is able to greatly reduce inflammation levels by removing grains, dairy, sugar, and by emphasizing a healthier omega six to omega three ratio.

Another staunch supporter of the Paleo diet is Nell Stephenson, a nutrition and diet coach. After learning about the Paleo diet during 2004, Ms. Stephenson found that it was the most significant change she has ever experienced. In awe over what this lifestyle can accomplish, she wrote to Dr. Cordain to share with him how it had both helped her and her clients.

It wasn't long before Dr. Cordain replied to her, and after communicating back and forth he even asked her to contribute to his official newsletter. The continued to write Paleo diet plants together, and during 2010, they co-wrote a cookbook.

During this time, Ms. Stephenson has been integrating parts of the Paleo lifestyle into her clients' nutrition. All of her clients, despite their variety of health concerns and conditions, soon found that they began to feel better, experienced an increase in health, and reached better weights.

While Ms. Stephenson had previously only been an average participant in triathlons, she greatly improved upon starting the Paleo lifestyle. Not only did her recovery time improve, but her training did, as well. She has now been able to win a spot in the World Championships in Kona. Not just once, but on eight occasions. While training she is continuing to spread the benefits of the Paleo lifestyle and is integrating it into her client's daily lives all around the world.

But why am I telling you about Ms. Stephenson? Not only is she a well-acclaimed nutrition coach who has helped countless people with her knowledge of the Paleo diet, but she has experienced its help firsthand.

When Ms. Stephenson grew up it was the 70s, which meant that she ate real whole foods. Much of her family's food was grown in their own garden and then cooked by her mother's hands. As a child, Stephenson had never even heard of a cookie. Upon watching Sesame Street, she asked her mother what Cookie Monster was eating. Her mother's response was that he had been eating a potato cookie, which resulted in her baking a potato and cutting it into circles to look like cookies.

Despite the in-season, local, organic, and wild diet and all of the anti-inflammatory and nourishing benefits it contained, Stephenson was frequently ill with her stomach. This went back as far as her infancy when she was taken to the pediatrician due to her regular digestion difficulties.

However, none of her doctors were able to learn what was aggravating her stomach. The most that they could assume was that she had a 'sensitive stomach'. This meant that as Stephenson grew up, she was well acquainted with having frequent stomach pain. Still, she stayed active most of her childhood with swimming, running, and other sports.

But then, the pain began to worsen. This resulted in frequent appointments with various specialists and several difficult emergency room trips. She experienced much physical and emotional pain during this time. Both from the stomach symptoms and the isolation that they caused. There were many times she would be unable to leave the house, or even the bathroom, due to the severity.

She was given some ridiculous medical advice, such as replacing vegetables with white rice in her diet and experienced a number of misdiagnoses. The doctors would assume that she must have irritable bowel syndrome, Crohn's, or colitis. They would put her on a list of medications without ever asking what her diet consisted of.

Stephenson got into endurance training, but she was experiencing her debilitating symptoms on a daily basis. This would interfere with both her training and racing. She would frequently have to stop competing or training in order to search for the nearest bathroom.

It got to the point where Stephenson could no longer allow it to control her life without answers. She took research into her own hands.

She tried fully committing to the vegan lifestyle. She even had a top-ten list of reasons why the vegan diet was the 'only' option. While she was including organic whole food ingredients such as coconut, sprouted nuts and seeds, and an abundance of vegetables, she was also consuming large amounts of soy and grains.

Yet, after six months on the vegan lifestyle, Stephenson would find herself waking up to dreams of eating fish, which lead to her feeling guilty. She tried to stay on the vegan diet, and she was able to maintain it. For two years. Then, she began to eat fish again.

It took her another year or two, but she once again once again began to eat meat from animals other than fish. She had come to the realization that it's important to support humane local, grass-fed, and free-range meat providers rather than the large inhumane companies. She learned the difference of grass-fed beef over feedlot beef on both the human body and the environment. And finally, she educated herself on whether or not it's ethical to consume animals.

Slowly, she introduced more wild-caught fish into her diet and found that she was both more energetic and recovering better from training. Yet, her stomach distress still remained.

Stephenson was desperate for answers. During the early 2000s, before many people were aware of gluten sensitivity and Celiac disease, she asked her doctor to run a blood test on Celiac. But her tests were negative. The gastroenterologist stressed that he didn't believe she should remove gluten from her diet. Then, he prescribed her Prozac and sent her away.

She couldn't take it anymore, Stephenson knew that her food and stomach symptoms must have been related somehow. But where to start? She would look into anything on diet and health, trying to find answers. Trying to find what had been causing her pain her entire life. During this research, Stephenson came across the Paleo diet, and how many of the illnesses in our modern society are caused by what we eat.

She soon learned how many of the foods that are standard in the American diet didn't even exist a little further back in our history. Our diets are leading to chronic inflammation, obesity, high blood pressure, diabetes, and autoimmune conditions. Many people are even suffering from a host of symptoms of their diets, despite not having a chronic illness. These people live constantly tired, their brain in a fog, undiagnosed stomach pains, and many other symptoms. But since nearly everyone else feels this way we figure it must be normal.

Rather than fully living, our diets are keeping us in a state of survival.

Within a few days of integrating the Paleo diet into her lifestyle, Stephenson's health began to make a marked improvement. She soon realized that even if her symptoms began as a kid due to the high content of whole grains in her diet, it definitely worsened while vegan. Between the faux meat, sprouted grains, and high soy content her gut health had been greatly damaged.

She now finds herself enjoying better health than ever before. She indulges in local seasonal produce, healthy sources of fat, and humanely sourced meats and fish. She has found her own balance with a Paleo lifestyle and has found it to be easily maintained during her many years on the plan.

Stephenson is now forty-four and enjoying life to the fullest, all because she is enjoying healthy whole foods that our bodies have known how to eat ever since ancient times. She has used her journey of ill health to full health to spread awareness, educate, and empower others on the effects of our food. Just like Nell Stephenson, you can take a step towards better health. You never know how much it can improve your life until you try.

The Paleolithic lifestyle may be quite different from what you are used to, especially if you eat the Standard American Diet or follow a vegan diet. But if you give it a chance, you will soon learn first-hand its many amazing benefits. You can experience increased mental and physical energy, improved gut health, reduced risk of disease, improved weight, and much more.

You have nothing to lose but everything to gain.

Chapter 2: The Paleo Diet and a Healthier You

There are many benefits to the Paleolithic diet, yet, many doctors have little to no education, awareness, or understanding of the issue. In fact, there are many doctors who see no problem with a diet full of sugar, refined grains, preservatives, and other harmful substances as long as the patient isn't obese or have diabetes. The problem is so severe that many doctors don't even understand the need to eat a healthy diet when treating cancer.

This understandably leads to much frustration in patients who are on the Paleo diet. A person's doctor is supposed to help guide them to better health. But how can a doctor do that when they are ignorant about basic nutrition? A doctor may think that all saturated fats are unhealthy, yet recommend a diet full of refined carbohydrates. They may promote artificial sweeteners and dairy, despite studies showing that these ingredients do more harm than good. Yet, many people still need a medical opinion about their dietary guidelines. This is especially true for people who suffer from diseases such as cancer, diabetes, high blood pressure, liver disease, heart disease, and more.

But just because your doctor is currently unaware of the benefits of the Paleolithic diet doesn't mean all hope is lost. There are many doctors out there who have seen and believe in this lifestyle. You can help your doctor help you and others by sharing the knowledge you have learned. One of the ways you can do this is to let your doctor see first-hand the benefits it has on you. If your doctor sees that the Paleo lifestyle helps you to lose weight, gain control over your blood sugar and blood pressure, and decrease other symptoms, they are likely to research the diet. This could even lead to your doctor suggesting the Paleolithic diet to other patients of theirs with similar conditions.

If your doctor is interested in learning more, you could always recommend your favorite book (such as this one), Dr. Loren Cordain's website, and scientific studies proving its benefits.

Due to false ideas purported in the late 1900s and early 2000s, some doctors may still believe that fats, especially saturated fats, are bad for you. But if you are able to show them studies and research that prove otherwise, they are more likely to feel confident about your new lifestyle. Remember, your doctor wants the best for you, but they may simply be operating on outdated information on nutrition. If your doctor is willing to learn the newest research, then they can better help you.

But if your doctor is completely unwilling to learn about the Paleolithic diet or work with you on your diet, then you may need to find a new doctor. Don't get me wrong, if a doctor has good reason to believe the Paleo diet won't work for you, then you should listen to them. Your doctor will know your individual condition and what might or might not work for you. But the truth is that many doctors are no longer taught about nutrition, so they simply stick to the damaging national nutritional recommendation. Many doctors are unwilling to learn about better health through the use of diet, they simply want to prescribe drugs as an easy fix. This is because a recent survey found that eighty-one percent of doctors are either working at full capacity or overextended.

In June of 2014, the American College of Sports Medicine, Bipartisan Policy Center, and the Alliance for a Healthier Generation claimed that doctors in America are not educating their patients on exercise, weight, and diet. They found that the reason for this is because many doctors themselves are not educated on these matters. Doctors need more training, but it can't be as simple as a one or two-hour class. There needs to be a large focus in medical school on how our lifestyles affect our health.

In all matters of our health, diet and otherwise, it is important to have a doctor who will listen to our needs, desires, and work together with us to find the best solution. A doctor who is overly busy and will just throw drug prescription after prescription at you without ever listening to you or fully analyzing you is unable to help.

It can be scary to have a doctor you can't trust. Your health is important, and you need them to put in the time that you deserve. Especially when these appointments are expensive, require us to take time off work, and are emotionally raw. Whatever reason you are seeing your doctor for, you deserve proper care, time, and attention. You deserve a doctor who will help you in your fight for better health and will help you feel at ease. Don't let a doctor make you feel as if your own health isn't your business. You deserve to have full control over your health. Here are some tips to help you in the process:

- Interview your doctor. Remember, you are paying your doctor to help care for your health. You have the right to question them and learn if you are both on the same page. For instance, if you would rather try natural treatments before drugs, you can ask your doctor their opinion on the matter. It is important to have a doctor that you feel comfortable talking with.

- If something your doctor says doesn't feel right, you don't have to trust it. Some doctors may think they are infallible, yet everyday people are misdiagnosed, given the wrong medication, and given inaccurate advice. One real-life example of this is from my own childhood. After swallowing a coin, one of the local doctors in our small town said I would need surgery to remove it. My parents were scared, but they scheduled the surgery. Thankfully, before the surgery, they took me into my regular family doctor. This doctor was shocked that the emergency room doctor wanted to do surgery because this is usually only done when children swallow batteries or sharp objects. Sure enough, my family doctor was right, and before long the coin passed through my system. No surgery needed!

So, if something makes you feel as if you can't quite trust what your doctor is saying, don't be afraid to get a second opinion.

- Does your doctor regularly consume a double bacon cheeseburger complete with a large soda and a side of fries? Maybe they even smoke. While these things are common, if your doctor regularly lives such an unhealthy lifestyle, you may want to consider that they may not be the best person to weigh in on what constitutes a healthy diet. After all, if you were hiring someone to give you business advice, would you rather someone who was in debt and struggling to get by or someone who was successfully running a business? The profession may be different, but the principle is the same.

- If you are hoping to find a new doctor, try asking local friends and family for recommendations. You can also check the list of approved doctors from your insurance company, or look online and find testimonies to help you choose who to see.

- Trust in your gut. If you feel as if something isn't quite right with a doctor, there is no harm in looking around for a new one. You won't hurt their feelings. Your short-term and long-term health is more important than a fake sense of peace with a doctor you feel uneasy with.

If you are having a difficult time finding a doctor who is well-versed in nutrition, then you may want to try seeing a nutritionist or a registered dietitian. Their job is literally to understand a variety of diets, how to incorporate them into your lifestyle, and whether or not it will help or hinder your health.

By seeing a nutritionist, you can find someone who is up-to-date on all the current information for a healthy lifestyle. They will be able to support you and help you know to transition onto the Paleo diet seamlessly. Many nutritionists will help their clients with recipes, meal planning, and grocery lists.

They may even be able to recommend the best places to shop locally. If you are chronically ill or have a disease, they can also help you to learn which foods to increase in your diet and which to avoid.

Rather than spending ten minutes with you and writing a prescription, a nutritionist will often spend an hour with their clients in an initial consultation. This gives them the ability to fully analyze your health, lifestyle, and symptoms so that they can make the best plan for you.

The Health Benefits of Paleo

Many people begin the Paleo diet hoping to lose weight, and while it can aid in weight loss, it is not specifically a weight-loss "diet." When on the Paleo lifestyle, it is important to look at the big picture rather than short-term results. Crash diets may help you lose more weight in less time, but they do this by ruining your health, wrecking your metabolism, and leading you into greater weight gain in the future. On the other hand, the Paleo lifestyle can help you naturally lose weight by reducing foods that can attack your gut, increase insulin resistance, and boost inflammation such as sugar, grains, and dairy.

Goals can be incredibly motivating, especially when you are beginning a new lifestyle. These goals can keep you enthusiastic and remind you of why you have chosen this when moments become difficult.

But you need to be careful when creating goals for weight loss. You don't want to have unrealistic expectations of yourself and how quickly you will lose weight. This is especially true if you are used to dieting. Remember, the Paleo diet has been shown to help with long-term sustained weight loss. This weight loss may take more time to achieve than weight loss with a crash diet, but it will be a more successful and healthy form of losing weight.

Don't let the scale rule you. These numbers aren't even a perfect way of tracking weight and tell you nothing about health. If you begin to feel frustrated, remind yourself of your goals. A goal to live a better life, to feel better, to increase your health, to enjoy better food, and to reach a sustainable weight.

But what exactly can you expect in regard to weight loss on the Paleolithic lifestyle?

Firstly, it is important to know that your weight is not linear. You are not going to lose exactly two or three pounds every week. In fact, the human body can adjust how much it weighs within five pounds during a single day. This is largely due to water weight, but there are many factors that can contribute to it. It can also change greatly depending on menstrual cycles. If you notice small fluctuations on the scale from day to day, it is nothing to worry about. Rather than tracking day to day, track your overall progress from week to week or month to month.

During your first week on the Paleo diet, you can expect rapid weight loss, anywhere between five to ten pounds. Though, depending on your previous lifestyle and health, the weight loss during the first week may be gradual or stalled.

Most people experience this weight loss due to our high-carbohydrate and grain filled diets. Each gram of carbohydrates in our body can hold onto three or four times its weight in water. This results in rapid water weight loss when you greatly reduce your grain intake. This effect is neither good or bad, it is simply a neutral effect of a low-carbohydrate diet.

After your initial week on Paleo, the weight loss should become more gradual. This is due to your body already expelling all of its excess water weight, and it is now slowly working at burning off your fat.

This is not something to be discouraged about, it is a good sign that your body is losing weight healthfully!

Your weight loss doesn't slow down because you are eating incorrectly, making mistakes, or following the Paleo lifestyle incorrectly. For some people, it simply takes time for the diet to help heal their body before they can lose weight. After a life eating processed foods, grains, sugar, dairy, and legumes your hormones could be altered from their ideal, you could have mild insulin resistance, you may not be sleeping well, there is a long list of reasons as to why your body may need to heal. Give it some time, and you will see progress.

If you have been on the Paleo diet for a long time and find you are not losing weight, you may want to look to see how many natural sugars and calories you are consuming. While most people don't count calories on the Paleo lifestyle, if you are eating a large amount of fruit, seeds, and nuts your weight can easily stall. These foods should be eaten in moderation.

If your doctor believes you are physically healthy enough to exercise, you may also want to try including some workouts into your life. Remember, the human body isn't meant to sit twenty-four/seven.

You don't have to believe me. Studies have shown that the Paleolithic diet is helpful to regain a metabolic balance and achieve sustained weight loss. In one study, seventy postmenopausal obese women were placed on two different diets for a two-year period. One group was allowed to eat as much Paleo food as they wished, whereas the other group maintained a Nordic Nutritional Recommendation diet, otherwise known as NNR. While both groups of women lost weight, the group on the Paleo diet experienced a significantly higher decrease in stomach fat loss. This group also had a more significant decrease in blood triglyceride levels. Overall, the Paleo group experienced many more benefits than the NNR group.

A study published in the European Journal of Clinical Nutrition studied the effects of the Paleo diet on healthy individuals. During only three weeks on the diet, not only did the participants experience a decrease in overall body weight, but their fat composition improved as did their waist circumference. Some other changes noted during the three weeks were improved blood pressure, improved antioxidant levels, and a more optimal ratio of potassium to sodium.

In another study, published in the autumn of 2015 by The American Journal of Clinical Nutrition, examined if the Paleo diet can reduce the risk of disease. This study found that the participants experienced improved weight loss and waist circumference over the control group. They also benefited from reduced blood triglycerides, lower blood pressure, lower cholesterol, and improved blood sugar. Even better, is that there were no adverse effects caused by the Paleo diet.

One of the leading diseases plaguing America is type II diabetes. This condition is worsened by the large amount of junk food, refined sugars, and grains in the American diet. Because of this, over thirty million people in the country have diabetes. This number is a staggering ten percent of the population! But America is not the only country suffering from diabetes. As more countries adopt America's love of junk food, their rates of diabetes are rising, as well.

In a diet studying the effects of the Paleo diet on patients with type II diabetes who are not being treated with insulin, the results were quite promising. Most of the participants had been living with diagnosed diabetes for an average of nine years. After being on the Paleo lifestyle for three months, the participants had greatly improved their glycemic control and risk factors for heart disease. It was found that the Paleo lifestyle was even more effective in the treatment of diabetes than the standard Diabetes diet.

One non-human study hoped to examine the difference between a Paleo diet and a grain diet on pigs. This study tracked glucose levels, insulin responses, blood pressure, and more. The researchers kept a close eye on the pigs' health prior to and during the course of the study. By the end, the group that ate a Paleo diet weighted twenty-two percent less and had forty-three percent of dangerous (subcutaneous) fat. The pigs experienced a great improvement in insulin, blood pressure, C-reactive protein, and more. The results were significant, and greatly showed the benefits of the Paleo diet. While this study is on pigs, other studies have proven that these effects cross over to humans.

There are many types of autoimmune disease prevalent in modern society. Some of these include rheumatoid arthritis, Celiac disease, multiple sclerosis, type I diabetes, inflammatory bowel disease, and more. These conditions are caused when the immune system is unable to distinguish your own body against foreign invaders. Your immune system begins to believe that your own cells and organs are bacteria or viruses that can cause harm. Therefore, your immune system will attack your own cells in the same way it would attack the bacteria. By attacking its own cells, your body will begin to destroy itself, causing further illness.

While the exact cause of autoimmune illnesses is unknown, it has been shown that our genetics, environment, and our gut all play a role in whether or not we develop these conditions.

But can we reduce our risk of developing and the severity of autoimmune illness even if we don't know the exact cause? Well, science says that we can, with the use of diet. The environmental factors that may impact our immune health include our diet. It is reasonable to assume that a diet full of whole foods would be better for our immune health than the proven detrimental Standard American Diet.

In the treatment of rheumatoid arthritis, diet has been especially successful. In this condition, the immune system will attack the body's own joints, causing inflammation and pain. The inflammation then causes the body to further attack itself, turning it into a terrible cycle.

Thankfully, the Paleo diet is well-known to help decrease inflammation. Not only does it decrease inflammatory foods such as processed foods, refined sugar, grains, dairy, and legumes, but it increases foods that naturally reduce inflammation.

In one study, participants with rheumatoid arthritis who followed the Dietary Guidelines for America had a thirty-three percent reduced the risk of rheumatoid arthritis. This is encouraging, especially since it indicates that if someone consumes an even healthier diet full of whole anti-inflammatory foods, they might be able to further reduce this risk.

The Paleo diet has been shown to greatly improve gut health, which can, in turn, improve autoimmune illnesses, as well. High levels of vitamin A and D from fatty fish, shellfish, and liver can support the regeneration of the gut lining. This is especially important because these fat-soluble vitamins are essential in the treatment of autoimmune disease. In fact, low levels of these two vitamins is a precursor to every type of autoimmune diseases, as well as allergic illnesses such as asthma.

Having the correct ratio of omega three to omega six is vital for health. With this out of balance not only does our inflammation increase but our risk of disease increases, as well. During the Paleolithic period people would consume the ideal portion, one part omega three to one part omega six. But people consuming the Standard American Diet have developed a ratio that is shockingly out of balance. This ratio is now as disproportionate as being twenty-five parts omega six to only one part omega three. Thankfully, by including more fatty fish and grass-fed meats we can once again regain the balance we need. This, in turn, helps to manage and prevent autoimmune disease.

Another known cause for autoimmune disease is oxidants. These cause damage to our cells and even promote cancer. On the other hand, many fruits and vegetables are full of antioxidants, which directly counter the damaging oxidants. These antioxidants are especially found in high quantities in bright and colorful plants, such as carrots, red bell peppers, purple cabbage, grapes, and oranges.

When eating fruit, it is important to remember that many of these oxidants occur in the peel of the fruit. Therefore, when possible try to consume the whole fruit, peel and all. Apples are a wonderful example of a fruit whose main nutrients lie within the peel.

In our throats, below our larynx, our thyroid gland lies. It may be only a small gland, but the unassuming thyroid is one of the most important components of our endocrine system. This system regulates our entire hormonal balance. The reason so much importance is in the thyroid is that this gland controls how sensitive our body is to hormones. If it becomes dysfunctional, then it can impede weight loss, affect our heart health, and even cause infertility.

There are many factors that may disrupt the thyroid and its hormones, which can cause either a lack of the needed hormones or an excess of the hormones. Both of these conditions have serious effects, and they are known as hypothyroidism and hyperthyroidism. People living with hypothyroidism regularly feel tired, fatigued, cold, and gain weight. It can even cause high cholesterol. On the other hand, people with hyperthyroidism often feel feverish, tired, and experience severe weight loss.

These problems are dangerous and regularly go undiagnosed for long lengths of time. Due to how vague the symptoms are and a lack of awareness, few patients will ask their doctors to run tests. Yet, most doctors won't test for thyroid issues unless the patient first requests it of them. If that wasn't bad enough, modern society is full of toxins and irritants that worsen the health of the thyroid, making these conditions more likely than ever. Thankfully, if we understand the thyroid and how it works, we can better care for it.

These thyroid dysfunctions are known to cause people to have sensitivities to many common foods. Some of the most common foods to disagree with thyroid conditions are soy, dairy, gluten, and eggs. Although, most of these foods are already eliminated on the Paleolithic diet.

One vital mineral for balanced thyroid function is iron. This mineral is naturally increased on the Paleo diet, due to the large amount of beef, fish, liver, poultry, ham, veal, and vegetables. These foods are also high in vital fatty acids, which can improve the thyroid.

While we may not yet fully understand what causes dysfunction of the thyroid, we do know that our environment and diets impact its functioning. If you are hoping to improve your thyroid health with the Paleo diet, you can simply follow the standard diet as you would for other health conditions. By eating this natural and balanced diet that is low in toxins we are able to improve our gut health, thereby improving our endocrine and thyroid health.

However, if you have been on the standard Paleo diet and you are still struggling with your thyroid or an autoimmune disease, there are other Paleo options. Dr. Izabella Wentz further customized the Paleo diet in order to increase its effectiveness for people with autoimmune disease. What is known as the Autoimmune Paleo Diet further removes foods that have been shown to add strain to the endocrine system and gut in these people. To follow the Autoimmune version of the Paleo diet simply remove these ingredients from your meals:

- Grains
- Gluten
- Processed Foods
- Soy
- Dairy
- Eggs
- Nuts and Seeds

- Sugars
- Beans and Legumes
- Nightshades
- Mushrooms
- Seaweed and Sea Vegetables
- Caffeine
- Alcohol
- High Glycemic Index Foods
- Canned Goods

Dr. Wentz promotes that this version may be more successful for some people, as these foods can bind to our endorphin receptors. Although, this version of the Paleo diet is more difficult. Therefore, Dr. Wentz recommends to first begin a gluten-free or standard Paleo diet, before slowly adjusting to and beginning the Autoimmune Paleo diet. By slowly eliminating these foods from your diet, you will find it much easier to adjust. Once fully beginning the Autoimmune Paleo diet, Dr. Wentz claims that you can begin to see the benefits within thirty to ninety days.

Chapter 3: Benefits of a Paleo Diet

The Paleo diet naturally aids in weight loss due to its high nutritional content, low sugar and grain content, and the lack of dairy. Although, some people will be at a loss due to a lack of weight loss. This is largely due to minor misunderstandings or mistakes that can impact a person's weight loss goal. Thankfully, with a few slight changes, you will find that you can easily and naturally lose weight at a healthy and sustained pace.

On the Paleo diet, you don't need to count calories. Yet, it is important to remember that these calories do still count, even if you do now know their number. It is important to understand how our body processes food and therefore the calories we eat. On the Paleo diet, we may be able to eat a higher caloric count than we did on the Standard American Diet and still, lose weight. This is not only because the sugars on the Standard American Diet cause insulin resistance and reduce our metabolism, but because they take less energy to digest. Whole foods, such as vegetables, take much more energy to simply digest and absorb, whereas a slice of cake takes little effort. This means that we can eat a higher number of calories in whole foods than junk food.

The problem comes in when people find ways to "cheat" without actually eating something non-Paleo. This is commonly seen in Paleo baked goods. People will bake with high quantities of almond and coconut flours, full-fat coconut milk, honey, dates, and maple syrup. While these are certainly healthier than a standard piece of cake, they are still rather calorie dense and take little energy to digest. Eating many baked goods such as these, even if Paleo, can impede weight loss. Therefore, try to save these sweet treats for every once in a while and special occasions rather than a regular occurrence.

If you are feeling overwhelmed by knowing that you are unable to eat grains, dairy, beans, sugar, or industrial seed oils on the Paleo diet, do not despair. Sure, you may not be able to eat some foods you are accustomed to, but you will learn to enjoy many delicious whole foods. Think about it, you will have the ability to enjoy a multitude of vegetables, fruits, meats, fish, seafood, herbs, and spices. These foods are completely Paleo and full of flavors. Rather than putting emphasis on what you are unable to eat, try fully enjoying the options that you do have. The glass is always better when seen as half full rather than half empty.

If you are regularly thinking of the foods you are unable to eat, you will find yourself miserable. Think of this as an opportunity to experience a new range of flavors, meals, and cuisines, as well as gain the health and weight you have always desired. You can always try new recipes, like the ones included in this book, and find new favorites.

Remember, this is a lifestyle, not a diet. You didn't gain weight overnight, and you won't lose it overnight, either. But by gradually losing weight at a balanced pace you will find it is much easier to sustain and you are unlike to gain those dreaded pounds back.

Everyone knows the story, whether they have experienced it themselves or seen someone else go through it. Someone starts a new diet, is amazed by losing ten or twenty pounds, and then their weight loss simply stalls. They don't lose a single additional pound. These people are often following the diet exactly the same way they had been in the beginning, yet they are having a weight loss stall for no discernible reason. It's incredibly frustrating and makes people want to give up. But before giving up, there is an important solution you most likely haven't tried. Five little letters can greatly affect your weight results. Sleep.

Due to hectic schedules, an overabundance of work and stress, blue lighting from TVs and smartphones, and bright indoor lighting many people have a disrupted circadian rhythm. This has greatly been shown to disrupt both our health and weight loss, yet many people are not taught this important factor.

A solid eight hours of sleep is recommended, though no less than seven and no more than nine is important. If we have either less or more sleep than this, then we can begin to experience chronic symptoms of sleep irregularity. This is most known to cause fatigue and a lack of weight loss, but it can also increase stress and many other symptoms.

To improve your sleep, and therefore your health and weight loss, try to practice good sleep hygiene. This means that you want to keep your bedroom cool. Limit time in bed to sleeping as much as possible. If you are unable to fall asleep within twenty to thirty minutes of lying in bed, then leave your bedroom until you feel you can fall asleep. Avoid stimulants such as caffeine within four hours of bed. Avoid the computer, phone, and TV within two hours of bedtime. Keep your bedroom completely dark with no lights when sleeping. Wake up at the same time every day. And, practice something relaxing such as reading or listening to calming music before bed.

Using good sleep hygiene takes practice and time to help, but there are many benefits. Not only will it improve your weight loss, but it will also decrease your risk of diseases down the road.

We often assume that losing weight requires a great deal of willpower. While willpower may play a role in living a healthy lifestyle and weight loss, it is needed much less than people believe. This misconception is largely because crash dieting causes much fatigue, nutritional deficiencies, and a sense of missing out, requiring willpower to maintain it. On the other hand, the Paleo lifestyle is full of delicious foods that you can enjoy. Steak, shrimp, sweet potatoes, berries, nuts, spices, and more are all allowed without caloric restriction!

Rather, a large problem when dieting, no matter if it's the Paleo lifestyle or another diet, is mindless eating. If we are watching TV, we can easily enjoy quite a large number of potato chips, french fries, cookies, or other foods. This isn't because of a lack of willpower, but rather because we are distracted. You haven't failed, you simply need to find a new way to enjoy snacking.

Instead of sitting with a big bag of potato chips or a bowl of cookies and mindlessly snacking, allow yourself to fully enjoy these snacks. You can consciously eat them, allowing yourself to savor the flavors. Yet, if you don't want to give up snacking while watching TV or reading a book, you can always portion out your snack into a single serving beforehand. This will ensure you don't accidentally overeat.

Know your goals. You may know that you want to lose weight, but why do you want to lose weight? Is it because you want to increase your health? Live a happier life? Become more active? Improve your sleep? Get better in bed? Walk up a flight of stairs without getting dizzy and out of breath?

There are many reasons we may want to lose weight. If you find your true goal behind your desire for weight loss, you can better help yourself attain it. Not only that, but you will find yourself more motivated and have an easier time tracking your progress.

Along with having benefits for weight loss, the Paleo diet is also high in nutrients. This is not only beneficial for people who are deficient in one or more of these important nutrients, but for everyone. This is because many people, even if they aren't deficient, are still not getting an adequate amount of these vitamins and minerals. This leads not only to general symptoms of fatigue, sleepiness, pain, and more but even to disease.

The Paleolithic lifestyle is found to be especially high in some of the most important nutrients missing from many Americans' diets.

Iron

This vital mineral is found in our blood, more specifically in our hemoglobin. The purpose of this is to carry oxygen from our lungs and to our red blood cells. Iron sustains our very lives, as well as being used for cellular functioning, the production of hormones and connective tissue, and growth.

What many people are unaware of is that there are two types of iron. This mineral comes in both heme and non-heme. While heme iron is easily absorbed by the body, non-heme iron is more difficult to absorb. This non-heme iron is found in plant-based foods but is often inhibited from being blocked. If that wasn't bad enough, non-heme iron may block the absorption of other minerals.

Thankfully, heme iron which is found in seafood and meats is easily absorbed, and unlike non-heme iron, it doesn't block the absorption of other minerals.

People who are most likely to have inadequate levels of iron include children, adolescents, people with heavy menstrual bleeding, and those who are pregnant. Although, certain medications and diseases such as cancer, heart disease, and inflammatory disease may also interfere with iron levels.

While an iron deficiency, known as anemia, is less common, it is highly concerning when it does occur. The people who are most likely to have anemia are those with a malabsorption condition, poor nutrition, or blood loss.

Calcium

We are told our entire lives of the importance of dairy. That we will develop a disease and fragile bones if we don't drink milk on a daily basis. But while many people rely on dairy products for dairy, this is in fact counterproductive. Studies have shown that higher rates of dairy actually cause more fragile bones, it has been doing the opposite of what we were originally taught!

However, calcium is still important for our bone health. Thankfully, there are many sources of calcium we can enjoy on the Paleo diet, completely dairy-free! Foods such as seaweed, sardines, collard greens, scallops, kale, broccoli, and bone broth all have high calcium levels.

Although, it is important that calcium alone is not well-absorbed. This is because vitamin D plays a vital role in its absorption. Thankfully, vitamin D can be found in high quantities on the Paleo lifestyle.

Likewise, sodium intake is low, which is beneficial since it has been found to hinder the absorption of calcium.

Iodine

One of the most important uses for iodine is the production of thyroid hormones. A deficiency in this mineral can cause hypothyroidism and thyroiditis, an autoimmune disease. This can affect our entire body, even our mental health, and fertility. A lack of iodine may cause dementia and infertility. For this reason, it is especially important for breastfeeding women to have sufficient iodine levels.

Thankfully, most Americans are not deficient in this mineral. But if you are unaware of where to get iodine in your diet, then you could easily become deficient once starting the Paleo lifestyle.

This isn't because the Paleo diet naturally contains much less of this mineral, but because many people receive their daily iodine requirements by fortification. Ever since the 1920s, America has been fortifying food with iodine. This was incredibly important, as up to seventy percent of the children had developed goiters due to deficiencies. This worked wonderfully because now iodine deficiencies are practically unheard of in the country.

But the foods most often containing iodine due to fortification or the production process are table salt, grains, and dairy. Trying to improve their health further, many people will switch to a healthy mineral-rich sea salt rather than table salt when going Paleo. But because of this they are no longer consuming any iodine fortified foods.

Thankfully, iodine can be naturally found in the American diet, you simply have to look for it. This mineral is commonly found in anything grown or raised in the sea, meaning fish, shellfish, and seafood. You can also get some iodine in produce that has been grown in soil that is rich in iodine. Although, this is no longer a reliable method because our soil has been depleted of many nutrients.

Some wonderful sources of iodine include turkey, fish, eggs, shellfish, dried seaweed, watercress, prunes, bananas, pineapple, and rhubarb.

Magnesium

While most people never consider the amount of magnesium they are getting in their diets, it is incredibly important. This is because this mineral affects over three hundred of our body's biological functions!

Magnesium is found in the bones and is important to maintain both their strength and integrity. The mineral improves digestion by relaxing the muscles found in the digestive tract. ATP is an important molecule that converts food into energy, magnesium affects this molecule. If we are deficient, we will become fatigued. Our mental health is affected by magnesium, as it can affect the production of the "happy hormone" serotonin, this can improve both anxiety and depression. Potassium and calcium are vital to helping our hearts beat regularly as well as the function of other muscles and nerves. But to work these minerals require the use of magnesium to regulate them within the body.

People who are most at risk for a magnesium deficiency are those on a highly-processed diet with little nutrition, malabsorption issues, digestive conditions, alcoholics, and those with chronically high-stress levels.

Thankfully, magnesium can be found in many whole foods, including those on the Paleolithic diet. Some of the options to increase your magnesium include spinach, pumpkin seeds, cashews, turnip greens, almonds, beet greens, sesame seeds, summer squash, sunflower seeds, and Swiss chard.

Folate

Also known as vitamin B9, folate is vital for shuttling molecules of carbon throughout the body. This process means that it affects our DNA; proteins; inflammation; the prevention of birth defects; and the prevention of cancer, Alzheimer's disease, and heart disease.

While people are encouraged to increase their folate levels when pregnant to prevent birth defects, there are still many misunderstandings about this vitamin. Firstly, the term 'folate' can apply to both a synthetic form of folate, known as folic acid and folate that is naturally found in foods.

Folic acid is often used to fortify foods and can be found in some supplements. Although, some higher quality supplements and vitamins have switched to using natural folate rather than folic acid. This is because while folic acid has previously been believed to be more easily absorbed by the body, it turns out this is somewhat untrue. Folic acid is absorbed in an estimated one-hundred percent, while folate is only absorbed in an estimated eighty percent.

Despite being better absorbed, our bodies must convert folic acid in order for it to be utilized as folate. Science has now learned that due to this conversion process is inefficient and slow. While the body is attempting to convert the folic acid, it circulates within the bloodstream. This is dangerous because when folic acid is dense within our bloodstream it can increase the risk of cancer and make vitamin B12 deficiencies more difficult to detect and diagnose.

On the other hand, there are multiple chemical forms of the natural folate found in food. This includes one that doesn't require the conversion process that folic acid must go through. Because of this, natural folate, while not as easily absorbed, is used much more efficiently and is safer.

While the most common cause of a folate deficiency is a lack of nutritional food, it can also be caused by smoking and alcoholism. A severe case of folate deficiency will cause the red blood cells to increase in size, underdeveloped, and decreases the total amount found within our blood.

It is best to consume both folate and vitamin C together. This is because when they are consumed simultaneously, our body is able to better absorb both vitamins.

Some Paleo folate options include broccoli, spinach, avocado, asparagus, lettuce, Brussels sprouts, papaya, mango, oranges, and sunflower seeds.

Potassium

One of the key minerals within our diets, potassium helps us to maintain many biological functions. This nutrient regulates blood pressure and heart rhythm, transports nutrients to the cells, controls muscle and nerve function, and maintains fluid balance. One of the main symptoms people will notice due to potassium deficiency is muscle cramps. Although, it can affect much more, including our kidneys and heart, without our realizing it.

This deficiency is most often found in people who are overweight, consume too much sodium, or have either heart or kidney illnesses. It is vital that we consume the correct proportions of potassium to sodium. Despite these two minerals working together in tandem, if we have the wrong ratio, we will develop a myriad of problems. Potassium levels should be much higher than sodium levels. But with the high sodium content found in most peoples' unhealthy diets, this ratio becomes highly off balance. The increase of sodium in our diet will then block the absorption of potassium.

Thankfully, the Paleo diet naturally increases the amount of potassium in our diet while reducing the amount of sodium we consume. Because of this, our Paleolithic ancestors were easily able to consume the correct balance of sodium to potassium.

Some foods which will increase your potassium levels include beets, avocado, butternut squash, sweet potatoes, salmon, pomegranate, sardines, broccoli, and Swiss chard.

Selenium

Selenium is an important mineral that is rich in antioxidants, yet it is often forgotten about. This mineral affects many of our natural proteins and enzymes, the synthesis of DNA, reproduction, as well as using its antioxidants to fight disease. Although, a shocking amount of people are deficient. It is estimated that worldwide one-billion people are affected by this deficiency.

Selenium also has a large impact on the human immune system. Not only does it protect us from viral infections, but it affects the cellular structure of our immune system. The T cells, killer T cells, and neutrophils in our immune system are vital for functioning, and this mineral affects all of them. But the benefits of selenium don't stop there. It greatly improves the absorption of vitamin E, may prevent cancer, lowers the risk of heart disease, and can protect against the toxic effects of mercury and arsenic.

With selenium's close ties to the immune system, it isn't surprising that selenium deficiencies are often linked to autoimmune disease and thyroid disorders. This deficiency is higher in people who live in areas where the soil is low in selenium levels, such a China. It can also be found in people with HIV, cancer, and those undergoing kidney dialysis.

Symptoms of this deficiency include reduced immune health, heart disease, dysfunctional cognitive health, and infertility. If you are worried you may be deficient, your doctor can run a blood test.

Some Paleo foods which are high in selenium include fish, shellfish, meat, eggs, mushrooms, onions, sunflower seeds, and Brazil nuts. The highest source within this list is Brazil nuts. Although, you don't want to consume more than four-hundred micrograms of selenium daily, otherwise you may develop a toxicity.

Vitamin A

Many people mistake vitamin A for beta-carotene, which is actually a precursor to vitamin A. This vitamin is essential for many biological functions, including the communication of our cells, vision health, a strong immune system, and healthy reproduction.

On the other hand, beta-carotene is a type of phytonutrient found within food. Phytonutrients are incredibly healing with anticancer and antioxidant properties, and are equally as important as vitamins and minerals. But in order to become an active form of vitamin A, beta-carotene has to be converted in an inefficient process.

Having normal levels of vitamin A is vital for the normal functioning of many of our systems. If we have low levels our digestion tract won't produce enough mucus enzymes to properly digest our food. Both female and male reproductive health relies on vitamin A. We are also more prone to autoimmune disease, infectious disease, thyroid dysfunction, bone disorders, and diseases of the eyes with inadequate levels.

Another note on beta-carotene, the vitamin A precursor, is that along with being ineffectively converted into vitamin A, it is also not as well absorbed. An average of only three percent of ingested beta-carotene is absorbed. So, while carrots and other plants may be wonderful sources of beta-carotene, you would do better-eating animal products. This is because animal products, such as meat and eggs, are the only source of true vitamin A that is easily absorbed.

While you need to be careful to get adequate levels of vitamin A, it is important not to consume too much while pregnant, otherwise, it may result in birth defects. As always, discuss this with your doctor.

The best sources of vitamin A include grass-fed meat and dairy products, liver, eggs, fish, and shellfish.

Vitamin D

While we may refer to this as a vitamin, it is actually a hormone which is important to many functions of our health. For instance, much emphasis is put on the importance of calcium for strong bones. But in order to effectively absorb calcium we also need vitamin D. Without adequate vitamin D we are likely to develop osteoporosis and broken bones.

Our mental health relies on vitamin D. You have most likely experienced, or at least heard of, people who become depressed during the winter months. This is largely due to the lack of sun proving us with less of this necessary nutrient. With a vitamin D deficiency, children's brains are unable to properly develop, brain function and our memory will deteriorate as we age, and it is even associated with depression and Alzheimer's disease.

Vitamin D is crucial for a healthy immune system and its function. Studies have even shown that lower levels of vitamin D are associated with autoimmune disease. One study found that with a vitamin D deficiency, patients with multiple sclerosis experienced worsening symptoms. Thankfully, by supplementing vitamin D, they found that the patients with the disease improved.

Some studies have even linked vitamin D to weight gain, cancer, and other diseases. This is especially worrisome when you consider that it has been shown that over forty-one percent of Americans are deficient in this important vitamin and hormone.

People who have come to the Paleo diet due to chronic illness should be especially conscientious of their vitamin D levels. Due to it being a fat-soluble vitamin, people with gut health disorders may be unable to fully absorb it. This means that people with Celiac disease, Crohn's Disease, Cystic fibrosis, ulcerative colitis, and certain types of liver disease are especially prone to vitamin D deficiencies.

People who are obese may also need increased doses of vitamin D since the fat stores will absorb much of it. In fact, one study found that people who are obese require forty percent more vitamin D than people who are at a healthy weight.

While some foods do contain vitamin D, it is important to keep in mind that unless you eat a lot of these foods you won't get enough. Although, the way that humans are designed to get vitamin D is through sunlight. If you are able to regularly spend time in the sun you should be okay. One study showed that a healthy adult is able to get most of their days' worth of vitamin D by spending between five to thirty minutes within direct sunlight. Yet, it is important to remember that sunscreen will prevent our bodies from absorbing this vitamin D.

If you find that you are unable to get enough vitamin D between your diet and sunlight, then you may want to consider taking a supplement. When consuming vitamin D in your diet, you can find it mostly in fish. But you should choose fish that is wild-caught. The best sources are salmon, mackerel, and herring.

Vitamin B12

Vitamin B12 is vital to nearly every chemical reaction within the body, as well as every cell. Yet, we are unable to produce this vitamin on our own, it must all come from our diet.

The production of our very DNA, the structure of all life, requires vitamin B12. If we have inadequate levels, then our cells will begin to swell. Along with playing an integral role in DNA, vitamin B12 is also vital to our neurotransmitters. These neurotransmitters are chemicals within the brain which enables the cells throughout our body and brain to communicate with one another.

Our mental health and mood regulation is reliant on this vitamin. Studies have shown that with chronically low levels of B12 our body will become unable to produce serotonin. But serotonin is a vital hormone to prevent depression. Some studies have even found that a deficiency may cause or worsen obsessive-compulsive disorder, otherwise known as OCD. A lack of this vitamin can even affect our sleep!

One of the first signs and symptoms of B12 deficiency is nerve damage. This usually first appears in the extremities, but eventually, it may affect the brain.

It is especially imperative to consume adequate levels of B12 while pregnant, both for yourself and your child. A scary sixty-two percent of pregnant women are deficient, so it is vital to talk with your doctor about consuming adequate vitamins and minerals.

Some of the best sources of vitamin B 12 includes tuna, salmon, scallops, lamb, and grass-fed beef.

Vitamin K

There are multiple forms of vitamin K, mainly K1 and K2. While vitamin K1, which is found in plants such as dark leafy greens, is well known, K2 is less known. But to get vitamin K2 we need to eat eggs, poultry, and dairy. Though, it can also be created through the process of fermentation.

Vitamin K is important for the necessary coagulation of blood, the formation of healthy bones and teeth, the protection of our arteries, and a reduced risk of cancer. It has even been found that vitamin K may play a role in the protection against Alzheimer's disease.

A clinical deficiency of vitamin K is rare in developed countries. Although, when it does occur it disrupts the coagulation of blood and causes bleeding gums, blood in the urine, nosebleeds, and heavy menstrual bleeding. The people most prone to this deficiency is those with liver disease or damage or people who are taking medicines such as Warfarin or Coumadin.

Yet, it is still possible to not have adequate levels of vitamin K without having a true deficiency, and this can cause its own problems. This can lead to osteoporosis, heart disease, and plaque buildup in the arteries.

To get more vitamin K2, consume more organ meats, eggs, dairy, sauerkraut, fish eggs, and natto.

Vitamin E

An important antioxidant, vitamin E protects our cells from oxidant damage. This in turns helps to protect us from cancer and other diseases. It can also reduce the aging of our cells, fight inflammation, protect the liver, and reduce the risk of developing heart disease. By increasing your vitamin E intake, you can also improve the moisture and elasticity of your skin, keeping it healthy and preventing skin disorders.

But there is generally not a need for vitamin E supplements on the Paleo diet, as there are several foods rich in it that you can enjoy. Some of these include spinach, almonds, avocado, sweet potato, and olive oil.

Vitamin B

Vitamin B6, also known as Pyridoxine, isn't talked about much. But it is important for healthy nerves and muscles as well as converting food into energy. Some other roles of B6 include the production of blood cells, insulin, and DNA.

Thankfully, vitamin B6 deficiencies are rare in developed countries, as it isn't difficult to attain. But some people who have poor absorption due to alcoholism or chronic diarrhea may develop a deficiency. This can result in skin disorders, anemia, fatigue, and seizures.

Even if someone doesn't have a medical deficiency of this vitamin, there are many conditions that may improve with a higher level of this vitamin. This is largely because even if you don't have a full-blown deficiency, it is still possible to not be meeting the daily recommendation. If you increase your consumption of B6 it is possible for it to improve asthma, PMS, high blood pressure, adrenal dysfunction, kidney stones, carpal tunnel syndrome, epilepsy, skin conditions, depression, and autism.

When consuming foods rich in vitamin B6, it is important to not add many acidic ingredients, otherwise, it can cause a breakdown in the vitamin. The process of freezing or canning foods with this vitamin may also cause it to degrade. Therefore, it is best to enjoy it in foods that are fresh and unprocessed.

Some of the best sources of vitamin B6 include tuna, liver, pistachios, bananas, summer squash, blackstrap molasses, and paprika.

Vitamin C

When flu and cold season comes around everyone hears the recommendation to get more vitamin C. People buy orange juice and supplements more than ever due to this vitamin's ability to boost the immune system. But a 2009 study concluded that if you increase your vitamin C levels only after showing symptoms, it won't help your cold. Instead, you need to regularly consume a high level of vitamin C, not only when you're sick. It may not completely prevent you from catching a cold or flu, but it could lessen the length and severity.

Thankfully, if you are eating fresh vegetables and fruits, then you shouldn't need supplementation. But the problem is that many people don't consume the daily recommendation of these important ingredients. Not only that but if the ingredients are cooked over high heat then it will destroy the vitamin C.

Due to the Paleo diet including a high concentration of fruits and vegetables, it is easy to get enough vitamin C, as long as you don't cook it any higher than medium heat. Remember, the fresher the produce the more vitamins it will have, as well.

The Paleolithic diet may help further by increasing your absorption of this vitamin. This is due to the Paleo diet being low in glucose, which is known to compete with vitamin C for absorption. People who have high blood sugar or regularly consume a high-carbohydrate diet are unlikely to increase their vitamin C by a significant amount.

Some of the best sources for vitamin C include bell peppers, guava, kiwi, strawberries, oranges, papaya, broccoli, tomatoes, snow peas, and kale.

Along with all of the nutritional benefits the Paleo diet has to offer from its wide array of vitamins, minerals, and phytonutrients, it also promotes an active lifestyle. The Paleo lifestyle encourages exercise under the same principles as it does in the diet. This means you can enjoy exercises that are designed after what our bodies were naturally built to do, similar to practices that were used during the Paleolithic period.

Yet, the exercise promoted by the Paleo lifestyle is different from that promoted throughout most of America and other countries. This means you aren't simply beginning your day with an hour at the gym. Instead, you can enjoy real-world physical activities that will strengthen your entire body.

By regularly exercising, you can improve your heart health, lower your risk of diabetes, strengthen your immune system, prevent osteoporosis, reduce the likelihood of stroke, and increase your longevity. Not only that, but it will prepare and strengthen your body for unpredictable situations and keep you healthy and vibrant as you age.

Not only does it improve your physical health, but living a more active lifestyle will improve your quality of life. It can do this by helping you to sleep better, reducing stress, improving sleep, strengthening your mind and memory, and you will better be able to enjoy physical activities of all kinds without getting dizzy and out of breath.

This doesn't mean there is a strict routine you have to follow to utilize a Paleolithic active lifestyle. Instead, you can utilize natural movements and activities rather than machine-based exercises in a gym. Brief and intense strength training rather than cardio. Ideally outdoor activities rather than indoor.

You are now well aware that whole grains, while supposedly healthy, are detrimental to your health. The same is true of cardio exercises. In fact, practicing cardio regularly increases your cortisol (the stress hormone) levels, damages the cells with damaging oxidants and free radicals, raises inflammation, and keeps your body in a mode of fight or flight. As if that weren't bad enough, large amounts of cardio often require a high-carbohydrate diet, which raises insulin levels.

Along with discouraging large amounts of cardio, the Paleolithic lifestyle encourages the use of proper rest and recovery time between workouts. Rather than practicing workouts that constantly leave you exhausted, store, and miserable, those on the Paleo lifestyle should leave you strengthened and energized. Why use an exercise that feels as if it's a form of torture, when you could instead live an enjoyable and energizing lifestyle? Exercise does not exist to ruin our lives, rather it should be used to improve it.

While there is no set way to live actively on the Paleolithic lifestyle, there are some broad guidelines that you can use to help you along the way. These can be easily personalized to each individual. If you find that one method doesn't work for you, then you can always try another.

During the Paleolithic period, people didn't go to a gym and use elliptical trainers and other machinery. People didn't work out a small group of muscles while ignoring the rest. There was no fitting workouts into a busy schedule as convenient. Yet, now people only go to the gym when it is convenient. And, when they do, they often workout a small group of muscles that aren't likely to be used outside of the gym. Our exercise has become disconnected from our lives, daily activities, and natural needs.

One of the proponents of moving as our bodies naturally intended is Erwan Le Corre, the founder of MovNat. You can get various workshops from him, which help us to rehabilitate and overcome the unhealthy way in which we are conditioned to exercise. Corre stresses the importance of the connection of our mind and body and relearning thirteen basic skills that we have forgotten. These thirteen skills are divided into three categories, including manipulative in which we move objects, combative which is used for self-defense, and locomotive which is used for moving ourselves.

MovNat offers a wide variety of resources, whether you want to take the workshop or go it alone. Simply begin to challenge yourself by doing natural activities outdoors, such as hiking, climbing a mountain, or climbing a tree.

One of the most well-known forms of exercise within the experienced Paleo social circles is CrossFit. The beauty of this routine is that it a variety of intense exercises that get your entire body moving, similarly to how they would in the Paleolithic period. CrossFit may be intense, but it can be customized to your individual skill level and athletic ability.

If you are worried about working out on your own, have no fear. If you join CrossFit you will receive personal coaching, tips, and encouragement. If you are unable to afford a membership, CrossFit regularly posts workouts on their website, which you can follow along with at home.

If you are not excited about the idea of a high-intensity workout, such as CrossFit, you may want to try the Primal Blueprint Fitness program. This program was started by the famed Mark Sisson, a well-known figure in the Paleo community. He described this program as "CrossFit for the rest of us." While both the Primal Blueprint Fitness program and CrossFit illustrate Paleolithic activity, they showcase it in different ways. Unlike CrossFit, The Primal Blueprint features slower movements, weight training, compound lifting, with the occasional high-intensity interval training (HIIT) and sprinting.

This program discourages the use of detrimental cardio and exercises which target only a set of muscles, and instead focuses on functional strength. Mark Sisson even encourages having fun while you exercise, rather than allowing it to be torture or an annoyance! You can have fun playing and doing fun activities, such as sports, while you exercise.

While CrossFit and the Primal Blueprint Fitness program focus on conditioning your entire body, there are other systems that are created to increase both strength and muscle mass by powerlifting. These programs include Leangains, Stronglifts, and Starting Strength.

All three of these programs share a few common features.

Rather than isolated exercises and machines, these programs encourage compound lifts and free weights. This is because utilizing compound lifts is more effective in building strength than isolated exercises. It is able to work a larger group of muscles, as well. Free weights are recommended over machines because they are more effective than spending hour after hour going from one machine to the next at the gym.

Instead of using lighter weights with many reps, they encourage fewer reps with heavier weights. This will help you to have more success and increase your strength effectively.

Even if you aren't a powerlifter, you can begin and enjoy the process of building muscles with this program. Even if you only have to start out at twenty or thirty pounds, that is okay! Everyone has to start somewhere, and before you know it you will be able to use heavier weights.

But the activity isn't the only important aspect of these exercise programs. Rest is an extremely important component, as well. Most people believe that the more exercise you put in the more benefits you will see. This is likely because they want to burn as many calories as possible to get slimmer. But on the Paleolithic diet, you aren't going to be living a lifestyle where you are constantly overeating and consuming a large level of carbohydrates. A cycle of the Standard American Diet with hours of cardio is nothing but detrimental.

Rest days are important to prevent injuries and to protect your immune system. But that is not all. When your body has a day to rest between workouts it is able to strengthen your muscles more than before. This is because the strengthening of muscles is a process of wearing them down by pushing them to their limits, and then allowing them time to knit back together. This can only happen though if you give them the time to heal and strengthen.

Remember, rest days don't delay your progress. On the contrary, by having two or three rest days a week you can increase the speed at which you improve and strengthen your body.

The Paleolithic diet is completely different from the Standard American Diet, and because of this people may be afraid that it will be difficult. After all, you will no longer be eating grains, sugar, or processed foods. But that doesn't mean that this way of eating is difficult. This way of eating is natural both to our bodies and lifestyles. It may take some adjustment, but once you have been on the Paleo diet for a short time you will find how easy it really is.

You can simply keep your fridge stocked with a variety of fresh fruits, vegetables, meat, and eggs; a pantry full of seasonings and herbs; and wild-caught fish and shellfish in the freezer to keep it as fresh as possible.

There are many delicious meals you can enjoy, even Paleo grain-free and dairy-free pizza! But if you want a quick and easy meal there are many ways you can accomplish this despite a busy schedule. It doesn't take long to steam a few vegetables, which you can then serve along with a side of chicken, pork, or beef. If you are in the mood for shellfish, it only takes ten to fifteen minutes to whip up some zucchini noodles with lemon pepper shrimp and bacon.

You can expect some cravings for sugar and other junk food the first week to up to a month, but within a few weeks, you will notice that you have no desire for these sickeningly sweet and processed foods any longer. Your body will come to crave the delicious whole foods that you can enjoy on a daily basis. You will love the avocado, mushrooms, berries, nuts, meats, and more!

Chapter 4: Potential Disadvantages of the Paleo Diet

The Paleolithic diet is great, you know that. You can enjoy eating in a way that is more natural to your body, promotes your health, boosts your energy, and can help you lose weight. You can also get rid of torturous exercise routines and replace them with a whole-body workout that is fun! But that doesn't mean there aren't some drawbacks. In this chapter, we will explore potential disadvantages of the Paleo diet and how you can overcome them.

There are many factors that affect how much the Paleo diet costs. It's not necessarily cheap, especially when you are buying organic. But that doesn't mean it has to be out of your price range, either.

The most expensive portion of the Paleo diet will be during the first week or two. This is because there are many staples that you likely don't already have on hand. You will need to completely restock your pantry, fridge, and freezer. But many of these ingredients will last much longer than a week, some may only need to be bought once a month. This includes ingredients such as coconut flour, almond butter, flaxseed, the food you buy in bulk, and more.

This is especially true if you choose to buy organic and grass-fed ingredients at Whole Foods. You want your ingredients to be as high-quality as possible. Studies have plainly shown that organic and grass-fed meat and eggs contain many more nutrients than their grain-fed versions. Not only that but if you are buying organic you won't be consuming all of the dangerous chemicals found in other ingredients.

However, this does not mean you can only enjoy the benefits of the Paleo diet if you aren't able to purchase an all organic diet. Instead, just purchase what you can afford organic. This may mean that you decide to buy organic meat, but non-organic vegetables. You may change which ingredients you buy organic and grass-fed week by week, depending on how much spare change you have.

Just because you are unable to buy organic grass-fed meat doesn't mean you have to go eat a bowl of macaroni and cheese or a Big Mac and fresh fries.

Instead, make your goals first to eat foods centered on the Paleo principles. Secondly, foods that are as clean as possible, such as being organic and grass-fed. Thirdly, food that is seasonal and local.

To save as much money as possible while eating Paleo, try one or all of these tips:

1. Look for meat that is on sale due to being near the expiration date. This can either be inexpensive meat or grass-fed meat. When you get home, you can tightly wrap it in plastic, then foil, and freeze it. This will prevent it from spoiling until you are able to use it.

2. Buy meat that has the skin on and bone in. Meat that has had this removed is much more expensive. You can either cook it with the bone and skin, or you can remove themselves before cooking. But there are benefits to keeping the bone and skin on your meat! It is incredibly tastier and the fat from the skin can keep you fuller for a longer period of time.

3. Learn to cook inexpensive meat products, such as liver and other organ meat. These may not be the most popular in this day and age, but during the Paleolithic period, they wouldn't have allowed a single scrap of meat to go to waste. Not only that, but organ meats are extremely nutritious and have many more nutrients than other cuts of meat. This includes vitamins and minerals such as iron, B12, and folate.

4. Reduce your intake of nuts. These wouldn't have been eaten in large quantities during the past, because it would take a lot of time and energy to collect them all and then remove the shells.

They are also really high in fat, which while healthy, can cause a stall in weight loss when eaten in high quantities. Nuts are a valuable resource. Savor them and slowly eat them rather than having them by the handful on a daily basis. This will not only help increase your weight loss, but it will save you money, as well.

5. Berries are delicious and full of nutrition. But that doesn't mean they come cheap. Due to the difficulty in growing berries and the speed at which they spoil, they can be expensive. But frozen berries are much more economical. If you want your berries but need to save a buck, try buying frozen berries, instead.

6. Rather than just buying foods as you need them, try to keep your freezer well stocked. If you see a sale on vegetables or meat, you can store them in the freezer for lengths of time. Some foods will already be freezer ready, while others you may want to first repackage or cook before freezing. But this only makes it more convenient for last minute meals or when your budget might be tighter in the future.

7. Lastly, remember to weight out the cost to your wallet compared to the cost of your health. Sure, we can't completely forsake our wallets in this society. But if you can make some changes in other aspects of your life in order to better afford the Paleo diet, it may be well worth it. Do you want to age gradually losing your health and vitality, or do you want to continue loving and living life?

Another large concern is the lack of dairy and therefore a supposed lack of calcium. But as we mentioned in the previous chapter, there is evidence that shows that dairy is not helping with our country's large calcium deficiency. This is despite many people making an effort to include large amounts of dairy in their daily diet, especially in the form of milk and yogurt. In fact, dairy has been shown to have a negative impact on bone health. Despite the calcium, it contains, people who regularly consume dairy are more likely to develop osteoporosis.

It is also debatable how much calcium we require in our daily diets. The official guidelines provided by the American government recommends one-thousand to thirteen-hundred milligrams a day. Yet, some researchers believe that we may only really need six-hundred to eight-hundred milligrams to maintain healthy bones. However much calcium you consume, it is best to ensure that you get a minimum of eight-hundred milligrams a day, to be safe.

There are many people who love the Paleo diet and enjoy a variety of meats, seafood, vegetables, fruits, and tubers. But some of these people aren't necessarily eating the right ingredients to maintain calcium levels. This can be especially true of people who are being careful to not eat too many nuts or seeds, which are a good source of calcium.

Although by eliminating grains and legumes, your body may not need as much calcium as someone who is on the Standard American Diet. This is because grains and legumes both contain phytic acid. This acid will gather and then excrete various minerals that your body requires. By eliminating grains and legumes from your diet you will be able to absorb more of the calcium you are eating rather than having it dumped from your body.

While many people assume that dairy is the highest source of calcium, this is not true. In fact, collard greens have much more calcium than dairy products. You can also find it in dried figs, oranges, canned sardines with bones-in, canned salmon with bones-in, kale, broccoli, and almond milk.

If you are following the Paleo diet, it is simple to consume enough calcium. You just have to put in the forethought to make sure that you are eating the right ingredients and combining it with the consumption of vitamin D.

Once beginning the Paleolithic lifestyle some people may experience stomach distress, this could include bloating, pain, and diarrhea. If you are not prepared for this, it could be concerning. You don't want to begin a new lifestyle, only to find it doesn't agree with your stomach. But don't worry. These symptoms are usually only short-lived and will go away on their own. Otherwise, you can make a few small tweaks to decrease these symptoms.

One of the most common causes for this is simply dietary changes causing your digestive system to need time to adjust. When we adopt a new diet, it doesn't matter what it is, it is possible to experience changes in our digestion. This is especially true with the Paleo diet since it is much lower in carbohydrates than the Standard American Diet. This is especially known to change people's bowel movements, possibly sending them to the bathroom frequently for the first week on the diet.

An increase in fat may also be a reason for digestion difficulties and diarrhea. This is because the Standard American Diet contains an average of twenty to thirty-five percent fat from calories. On the other hand, people on the Paleo diet often get fifty to seventy-five percent of their calories from fat. By rapidly increasing the amount of fat you are eating your body may have a difficult time adjusting. This is due too it needing to produce more enzymes and bile to digest the fat. If you begin to have diarrhea, try cutting back on your fat intake and then slowly increasing it until you are able to more easily manage it without any side effects.

If you are eating an appropriate amount of fat another cause of diarrhea may be due to a high intake of short-chain fermentable carbohydrates. This type of carbohydrate is found in certain fruits, vegetables, and nuts that can be eaten on the Paleo lifestyle. For instance, apples, pears, mango, tomato paste, and asparagus all have high levels of fructose.

Foods such as peaches, watermelon, mushroom, avocado, and cauliflower all have something known as polyols. These are sugar alcohols, which do not actually contain alcohol but are a low-calorie sweetener. Most sugar-alcohols are man-made and added to diet foods, but some, such as polyols, are found naturally in certain foods. The problem with this is that sugar alcohols can cause problems in some people's digestion. While most people may be left unaffected, people with a more sensitive gut may develop pain and diarrhea. If you find yourself having a lot of stomach pain, ensure that you aren't eating these ingredients in overly large quantities.

A Paleo diet should have sufficient protein. But it is not a high-protein diet, but rather a high-fat diet. This means that if you are consuming more lean proteins rather than fattier cuts of meat you could be experiencing what is known as "rabbit starvation." This is caused because the body is unable to process having more than thirty or thirty-five percent of its calorie intake from protein. If you exceed this limit you are likely to experience muscle atrophy, fatigue, and diarrhea. To rectify this, try to enjoy fattier cuts of meat, such as beef, dark meat chicken, and salmon. Likewise, you can add in olive oil, coconut oil, nuts, seeds, and avocado.

If nothing about your diet seems off, you aren't eating too much protein, you aren't eating too much fat or short-chain fermentable carbohydrates, and you have been on the Paleolithic lifestyle for more than a few weeks, then you should discuss this with your doctor. It may not be your diet that is causing you discomfort and pain, rather a gastrointestinal condition.

Two of the biggest reasons people begin the Paleolithic lifestyle is to improve energy and other symptoms such as headaches. They get excited reading blogs, testimonials, books, and looking at recipes. But upon trying it themselves they find that they don't turn from a junk-food eating couch potato to an amazing athlete. Instead, they are simply struggling to know what to eat because they are tired and their head is pounding.

What could be causing this when you should be feeling better? There are a couple of obvious options. These are that you are sleeping poorly due to the drastic change, you quit caffeine, or you could have made some other life change that is affecting you. But if none of these are the cause, and it truly is the Paleo diet, you will be happy to know that this should be simple and easy to fix.

Firstly, during the first one to three weeks on a new diet, people often are going through a transition period. This is especially true of diets, such as Paleo, where you are altering your entire way of eating. After all, you are no longer eating grains, beans, sugar, or dairy! Not only that but in general you are eating a really low carbohydrate level.

For these first few weeks, it takes willpower, preparation, and routine in order to get through the alteration. Plan ahead so that you know what you want to eat, get into a routine so that you are sleeping well and eating regularly, and keep the willpower to at least allow yourself to try out the Paleo diet for a full month. At the end of that month, you should feel amazing.

Just look at diets such as Whole30 and the ketogenic diet as an example. Both of these diets are similarly difficult to begin as the Paleo lifestyle. People will often feel really drained and tired the first few weeks but after the initial month of adjusting they feel better than ever before.

Another cause of headaches, weakness, and fatigue could be having too few carbohydrates in your diet. Yet, this may sound odd considering it's a low-carbohydrate lifestyle without grains or legumes. But that doesn't mean you are supposed to completely eliminate carbohydrates. It is still important to get some into our daily diet.

It may be a little tricky, but with a little adjustment, you should be able to find your perfect carbohydrate balance on the Paleolithic lifestyle.

You don't want so much as to cause a sugar rush or insulin reaction. But you also don't want so little that you don't have enough energy to fuel your activity and mental health. Your muscles love to use carbohydrates for energy, so it is especially important to eat some before a high-intensity workout.

Some people simply feel better when they have a higher starch content in their diet. There isn't necessarily an explanation why some people need a higher starch level than others, though women, especially pregnant women, often do better with a slightly higher starch level. If you are one of these people you will likely find that if you up your starch intake that not only will your energy increase, but you will sleep better, wake up more refreshed, and your feet and hands will stop being constantly cold.

But how do you add in these starches without grains and legumes? Simply add in more potatoes, sweet potatoes, carrots, winter squash, plantains, bananas, and chestnuts.

Chapter 5: Your First Seven Days on the Paleo Diet

When beginning a new lifestyle, you need to know all of the reasons to begin, including anecdotal evidence, scientific evidence, historical evidence, and more. You have learned all of that. But you also need a simple and straightforward plan to get started. In this chapter, you will be provided with an overview of the foods that you can eat; those you shouldn't; and recipes that will keep you full, energized, and happy.

On the Paleo diet grains, legumes, and dairy are all avoided. This means that it is much lower in daily carbohydrate levels than the Standard American diet. But that doesn't mean you don't eat any carbohydrates, they are still important. Even without America's most loved sources of carbohydrates, there are many more options that are satisfying and delicious. As if that weren't enough, these ingredients are also full of vitamins, minerals, phytonutrients, and fiber.

What are these magical sources of carbohydrates? Well, these amazing sources of carbohydrates and nutrients? Fruits and vegetables!

These fruits and vegetables, the carbohydrates eaten by our Paleolithic ancestors, have a completely different impact on our bodies than grains and legumes. While grains and legumes cause damage to our digestive tract, fruits and vegetables can heal them. One may cause high blood sugar, but the other promotes balance. Carbohydrates themselves are not the enemy, their value depends upon their source.

Some people may benefit from a low-carbohydrate diet. People such as those with epilepsy, Alzheimer's disease, polycystic ovarian syndrome, Parkinson's disease, diabetes, and metabolic syndrome may benefit from a low-carbohydrate version of the Paleo diet. These people could combine both the Paleo diet and the Ketogenic diet for optimal health and success. This is because a low-carbohydrate diet has been found to help these people, and others with neurological conditions.

But while a low-carbohydrate may beneficial for people with neurological illnesses or a few select other conditions, the remainder of us can benefit from carbohydrates. In fact, one to three servings of nutritious starches a day can greatly increase energy and vitality. This is especially true for athletes and those with chronic fatigue.

Thankfully, there are a wide range of fruits we can enjoy, as well as both starchy and non-starchy vegetables. When choosing what to eat, you can always buy what is least expensive if you are on a tight budget. However, if you can afford it try to shop organically, and ideally locally and seasonally, as well.

It is best to choose fruits and vegetables that are all the colors of the rainbow rather than just green, solely orange, or little more than white. This is because different vitamin, antioxidant, and phytonutrients can be found in different colors of fruits and vegetables. Try to mix things up so that you can have a balanced supply of nutrition.

While there are many fruits and vegetables you can enjoy, let's look at some starchy options for when you need a boost of energy.

Sweet Potatoes:

One of the best options for a healthy starch source is sweet potatoes. These are both delicious and versatile. Whether you are making sweet potato fried, stuffing them, roasting them, making potato salad, or even using them as a substitute for bread

One of the many benefits of this fruit is that it is an excellent source of both soluble and insoluble fibers. This is ideal because it helps to regulate your digestive tract and gut health. The fiber can also help to prevent blood sugar spikes and lower cholesterol.

This root vegetable is full of nutrients. A single serving meets nearly three-hundred and eighty percent of your daily beta-carotene, which as you will remember is the precursor to vitamin A. Large quantities of vitamins B6, E, and C can be found, as well as the minerals copper, iron, potassium, and manganese. Now only do sweet potatoes have more vitamins and minerals than white potatoes, but they also have a lower glycemic index.

Along with the traditional orange sweet potatoes, you can also find Japanese purple sweet potatoes known as "ube" and a white sweet potato known as Hannah.

Beets:

While red beets are the most common option, you can also find golden beets and candy cane beets! If you've never heard of candy cane beets they also are known as Chioggia beets and pronounced as kee-OH-gee-uh. These beets originated in Northern Italy and the inside is stripped just like a candy cane!

Some people may think they don't like beets, but I urge you to give other varieties a try if you've only tried the traditional red beet. Golden beets are especially wonderful because they have a smoother flavor that is slightly sweeter and with a milder early flavor than red beets. You may also want to try the beets prepared in different ways. A salad topped with roasted or pickled golden beets is always delicious. You can add some diced beet to a smoothie for extra nutrition. Try adding some beets to tomato sauce to remove the acidity and increase its depth of flavor. You can even enjoy a salad made out of beet greens!

Beets are full of nutrition, including a variety of vitamins, minerals, phytonutrients, and antioxidants. This vegetable is rich in folate, which can increase the health of the brain and nervous system. They are also an excellent source for both calcium and magnesium.

Winter Squash:

Whether you enjoy pumpkin, butternut squash, spaghetti squash, acorn squash, buttercup squash, delicata squash, carnival squash, or kabocha squash, there are many wonderful winter squash varieties to enjoy. This selection of squash also offers you a variety of flavor, where some are sweet others are savory. You can enjoy these roasted with oil, salt, and garlic or with a bit of cinnamon and maple syrup. You can also make a creamy winter soup, make "spaghetti" and meatballs with spaghetti squash, or add them into any one of many of your favorite dishes. These squash truly are versatile.

In general, squash is lower in carbohydrates and calories than sweet potatoes. But some varieties such as butternut squash, offer a similar sweet flavor.

The exact nutrition of squash varies from variety to variety, while butternut is high in beta-carotene acorn is high in vitamin C. Try a variety of squash in order to also enjoy the many benefits they all have to offer.

You can even roast the seeds of squash, similarly to pumpkin seeds, and enjoy them as a treat! Not only can it be a tasty salted snack, but the chemicals are known as phytosterols found in these seeds help to lower cholesterol.

Plantains:

Those who are unfamiliar with plantains may think that they are the same as bananas. This makes sense because they look similar are a close relative to the banana, and have many of the same benefits.

Both plantains and bananas share a rich potassium content, as well as having the ability to boost the immune system. But plantains have many more benefits to enjoy. For one, they contain less sugar and more starch than a banana. This enables them to affect your blood sugar less and be more versatile while cooking. Plantains are also known for their fiber, beta-carotene, magnesium, and vitamin C.

While this fruit is greatly underappreciated in America, they are quite common in certain parts of the world. Still, they can easily be found in most grocery stores at a fair price. While they may be a fruit, they are often served in a savory setting as a vegetable. Plantains can even substitute potatoes or rice in some cases!

In South America, tostones are a popular Plantain dish, where the plantains are sliced, slightly smashed, and then fried. Plantain chips can also be a delicious baked or pan-fried alternative, as well as grilled plantains.

Tapioca:

Also known as cassava root, tapioca has become incredibly popular as a gluten and grain free option, especially in the Paleo community. Not only can tapioca be made into a delicious Paleo pudding, but it can be ground into a flour to cook and bake with. This is especially helpful for when you want to thicken sauces.

But many people don't know that tapioca is also high in protein, and minerals including magnesium, iron, zinc, copper, and manganese.

If you buy tapioca in its original cassava root form, found in the vegetable department, you can slice it thinly and then cook it into crispy chips. But remember, if you are hoping to use tapioca pearls or flour as a baking ingredient for puddings, bread, or cakes, you should keep it for rare special occasions.

Along with carbohydrates protein is extremely important. While low-fat diet may have been touted as the only healthy option for the past three decades, this opinion was greatly misinformed. After all, it was this low-fat dogma that leads the country into a major epidemic of obesity.

Thankfully, more people are beginning to see the benefits of healthy sources of protein-rich with fat. You don't have to stick to dry and flavorless chicken breasts. You can enjoy fatty cuts of beef, veal, pork, fish, and more.

While everyone has long agreed that protein is important, what exactly is it? Put simply, they are a type of molecule known as amino acids. There are twenty types of amino acids divided between three group types. Of these groups of amino acids, the first group is the most important and is known as the essential amino acids. These are proteins that your body is unable to produce on its own, and must receive from our diets.

These amino acids, therefore protein, plays many key roles in the body. They are the building blocks for our DNA, helping to maintain all of our cells. They affect our digestion, help the cells communicate with one another, affect our muscle movement, and much more.

It may sound daunting to consume all ten of the essential amino acids through your diet on a daily basis, thankfully it is not difficult. This is because meats and eggs contain all ten of these amino acids, making them a complete source of protein. Unlike on the vegan and vegetarian diets, on the Paleo lifestyle, you will have no problem getting all of the needed amino acids.

But how much protein do you need, exactly? Well, studies show that as long as ten percent of our daily caloric intake includes sources of complete protein then we will be meeting our amino acid needs. If we consume less than this, then we will begin to lose lean muscle, lose energy, experience decreased brain function, and more. Although, on the Paleolithic diet it is quite difficult to consume less than ten percent protein, anyways. You would have to be severely limiting your intake of meat and eggs, which most people won't do.

But this is only the minimum needed protein. You may be wondering how much protein is too much, and what the ideal amount is.

The body is unable to metabolize protein after thirty-five percent caloric intake. Because of this, a diet consisting of twenty to twenty-nine percent protein is considered a high protein diet. Someone eating thirty to thirty-nine percent protein is on a very high protein diet. This shows that the term "high protein" is relative.

Although, this percentage is based on a normal caloric intake of approximately two-thousand daily calories. The exact amount of protein you are consuming is important, as well. People can begin to develop protein toxicity when they are consuming more than two-hundred and thirty grams of protein in a day. It is incredibly dangerous to develop protein toxicity, thankfully it is also difficult to consume this amount of protein, so it is rare.

This means that a human can survive with anywhere between ten and thirty-five percent of their daily caloric intake being protein. That is, as long as this amount is no more than two hundred and thirty grams of protein or nine-hundred and twenty calories worth.

Yet, while we may be able to survive on these levels of protein, that does not mean anywhere within that range is ideal or can help us thrive. Thankfully, by looking at the Paleolithic period we can get an idea for how much the hunters and gathers would eat and how much we should consume.

It is believed that our ancestors would wisely choose to hunt the fattest animals so that they could gain more meat. Because of the higher fat content in these animals, their daily protein intake was most likely between fifteen and twenty percent of their caloric intake. This means that this range is most likely ideal for people who have no special medical or nutritional considerations. Of course, if you have a medical condition you should ask your doctor about your ideal level of protein intake.

You can always measure and weigh all of your protein sources to know you are getting the correct amount. But in general, this is not needed. Most of us are able to make an estimate of how much protein we are eating just by looking at the serving size and knowing how much protein that source of meat, fish, eggs, or nuts is known to contain.

Following is a list of some of the most popular Paleo protein sources and their protein levels.

- Three ounces of beef: twenty-four grams
- Three ounces of chicken: twenty-seven grams
- Three ounces of turkey: twenty-five grams
- Three ounces of ham: twenty-one grams
- Three ounces of lean pork: twenty-five grams
- Three ounces of canned tuna: twenty-three grams
- Three ounces of salmon: twenty-two grams
- Three ounces of shrimp: twenty-one grams
- One medium egg: six grams
- Half a cup of almonds: fifteen grams
- Half a cup of walnuts: ten grams
- Half a cup of cashews ten grams
- Half a cup of sunflower seeds: thirteen grams

What do you need aside from carbohydrates and protein? Fat! You now know that the fats found in meat and eggs, known as saturated fats, are not the enemy that they have been made out to be. But did you know they can even increase your brain health, make you happier, and increase your energy levels? This is because our bodies are designed to run off of fats as a primary energy source, but they are unable to do this on the Standard American Diet due to the overabundance of carbohydrate. These carbohydrates prevent the body from being able to utilize the fat we eat, so it begins to store this digested fat into body fat for use later on. But if we are eating a healthy amount of carbohydrates, as they did during the Paleolithic period, our body can produce a more efficient energy source out of these fats, known as ketones.

But sometimes people will get into a rut and constantly eat the same source of fat. Consider this, if the only vegetable you ever eat is broccoli you won't be healthy. This is because while broccoli has many benefits, it is unable to provide all of your nutritional needs. The same can be said for fat. If you only ever eat butter, then you will be missing out on the important benefits of other fats.

Firstly, you want to eliminate and sources of unhealthy fat within your diet. This includes vegetable oils that are high in polyunsaturated fats and omega six. Some of these unhealthy fats include soybean, corn, peanut, and grape seed oils. Don't let this list scare you, there are plenty of healthy and delicious fats you can enjoy.

Ghee:

Butter is not strictly Paleo, because the Paleolithic people didn't consume dairy. But if you warm the butter you can use a spoon and remove all of the dairy within it that floats to the top. You can then run it through a cheesecloth to completely remove any remaining dairy. This process is known as making clarified butter or ghee. While people who have extreme allergy conditions may not be able to consume ghee, most people are completely fine eating it. This is because both the lactose and casein have been removed. Even people with dairy allergies or sensitives frequently consume ghee.

This is a wonderful option because butter tastes good on anything and everything. Since ghee is a purified form of butter, it tastes even better.

This has many health benefits, including containing conjugated linoleic acid, also known as CLA. This type of fatty acid is wonderful because it has been shown to have anti-cancer properties.

When choosing butter you want grass-fed, which you can either get from your butcher. Although, KerryGold is a common brand of grass-fed butter found in most grocery stores.

Not only does grass-fed butter taste much better than the grain-fed varieties, but it's better for you, too. Studies have shown that grain-fed butter contains a significantly larger number of CLA fatty acid and vitamins. This includes vitamins such as A, E, and K.

Coconut Oil:

One of the favorite fat sources in the Paleo community is coconut oil, and there's a good reason for this. Firstly, coconut oil is ninety-two percent saturated fat, which means that it becomes solid at room temperature and won't easily burn under high heat.

But these saturated fats found in coconut have some even more amazing benefits. They have been shown to raise good cholesterol while lowering bad cholesterol.

A large percentage of the fats in coconut oil are medium-chain triglycerides, otherwise known as MCTs. While most fatty acids you consume in oils and meats are long-chain, meaning that the molecules have to be broken down before being digested, this is not the case with MCTs. Since MCTs are already a shortened version of fatty acids they are able to be digested more quickly, therefore providing a quick and efficient energy source.

A large portion of these MCTs can be turned into ketones, which is not only beneficial for energy and burning body fat, but it can also help neurological conditions. Many studies have shown that MCTs and ketones are able to help in treating Alzheimer's disease, multiple sclerosis, and much more.

Olive Oil:

Unlike the unhealthy vegetable oils mentioned earlier, olive oil is not an unhealthy option. In fact, olives aren't even a vegetable, they are a fruit! This oil is a healthy monounsaturated fat, but it is best to use it raw, not cooked. This is because olive oil can quickly burn and oxidize under heat. But olive oil is the perfect option when making salad dressings or to top an already cooked meal.

When choosing olive oil, it is best to buy extra virgin olive oil, as it has the most benefits. It is also best to buy olive oil that is in dark bottles, as this keeps the fats fresh longer. Once you buy it, store it in a dark and cool cabinet to prevent it from oxidizing as quickly. You can even store it in the refrigerator! Keep in mind, if you store it in the fridge it will become cloudy due to the fats becoming cold, but it will return to normal at room temperature.

Avocado Oil:

Like olives, many people consider avocados a vegetable, when they are in fact a fruit! While these can be enjoyed in the form of avocado oil, you can also enjoy the full fresh fruit. When served fresh these can be a wonderful accompaniment to any meal, but they can also be stuffed with eggs and roasted or baked into fries. The avocado oil is perfect for topping meals, making dressing, and in homemade mayonnaise.

There are many benefits to choosing avocados and their oil. They are high in oleic acid, which is an extremely healthy source of fat which is good for your heart health. They are also high in fiber, antioxidants, potassium, vitamin E, and a variety of B vitamins.

Animal Fats:

Whether you are enjoying fat from beef, duck, chicken, pork, fish, or more, it is the essence of the Paleo lifestyle. This is because our Paleolithic ancestors would eat large amounts of these animals, and others, for energy. Because of this, they got a large percentage of their fat intake from these meats. They were living a life in nature eating the foods that were naturally available and healthy.

Due to animal fats being highly saturated, they also provide the benefit of being able to cook at high temperatures and the ability to stay stable at room temperature. And, because these fats aren't overly popular, you can frequently buy them at an inexpensive price. Even the fats coming from well-treated and raised animals aren't overly expensive!

To get the best price on these fats to go straight to the butcher, who you can ask for lard from various animals or beef tallow. If your butcher doesn't have these rendered and ready to cook with you will need to render them yourself. Don't be afraid, it's very easy.

To make your lard or tallow ready to use you can by either unrefined lard or beef suet, both of which are inexpensive. You can then either render them using the wet or dry methods.

To use the dry method, you will remove any meat, blood, or veins from the fat before chopping it into small pieces. Afterward, you can place it in a heavy-bottomed Dutch oven or a crock-pot. If using the Dutch oven, place it over very low heat. If using the crockpot, place it on the low setting.

Continue to allow it to cook until all of the white pieces of fat turn into brown and dry. Carefully strain out the pure lard or tallow through a sieve and allow it to cool. The fat will be extremely hot and can burn you rather seriously, so be careful!

Once your lard or tallow is cooled you can cook with it at your leisure. It should set up hard and be white at this point.

Aside from these ingredients, you can enjoy eggs, nuts, and seeds. Although, you should be careful with nuts and seeds. This can be high in omega six fatty acids, which in large amounts can cause a disturbance in your omega six to omega three ratio. It can also increase inflammation and trigger digestive upset. Nuts and seeds are a healthy fat, but only in moderation.

Now you know what you can eat, but having a list of what you specifically shouldn't eat can be helpful, as well. Following is a list of the main non-Paleo foods that don't have a part in this healthy lifestyle. This is largely because these ingredients were not eaten by our Paleolithic ancestors, but also because studies have shown that they have specific compounds within them that can harm our health.

Grains and cereals:

All forms of grains and cereals should be avoided. This includes, but is not limited to, wheat, corn, barley, millet, rice, oats, sorghum, and rye.

Legumes:

All beans should be avoided, such as black beans, kidney beans, mung beans, lima beans, soybeans, and garbanzo beans. But legumes also include foods that aren't beans, therefore peanuts, sugar snap peas, lentils, and black-eyed peas are not allowed.

Dairy:

While clarified butter or ghee may be permuted, milk, regular butter, yogurt, cream cheese, sour cream, cheese, and other dairy products are prohibited.

Grain-Like Seeds:

This includes seeds such as quinoa, buckwheat, and amaranth.

Conventional Sweeteners:

While honey, maple syrup, coconut sap, coconut palm sugar, and dates may be allowed as the occasional sweet, other sweeteners are not allowed. This means no sugar, corn syrup, artificial sweeteners, sugar alcohols, or other sweeteners.

Soda and Juice:

Soda is obviously not allowed, because it is a processed food and also contains sugar. But all types of juice are prohibited, as well. This is because juice has had the fiber removed. Instead, choose to eat real whole fruits.

Factory Farmed Meats:

While some people simply may not be able to afford grass-fed and antibiotic-free meats, and that is okay, if you are able to afford the higher quality meats do so. This is because meat will be a large portion of your diet, and the nutritional value of the meat greatly varies based on how it was raised.

Processed Foods:

While processed foods are the standard American fare, they are extremely unhealthy. Avoid processed meats, fast food, chips, and other heavily processed ingredients. If a caveman didn't eat it, then you shouldn't either.

Paleo-Friendly Recipes

Just because you are following a new lifestyle doesn't mean it has to be difficult. Following is a list of simple and delicious breakfast, lunch, dinner, snack, and Instant Pot recipes, all completely Paleo-friendly!

Bacon Sweet Potato Skillet

One-pot meals are easy, especially considering it doesn't lead to a messy kitchen full of dishes to wash. This delicious meal if full of protein and vegetables that everyone will love. But it isn't just for breakfast. The sweet and salty combination from the bacon and sweet potatoes make it ideal for any meal.

Ingredients:
Sweet potatoes, peeled and diced into half-inch cubes – 5 cups
Zucchini, peeled and diced – 4 cups
Red bell pepper, diced – 1 cup
Onion, diced – 1 cup
Large eggs – 6
Bacon, cut chopped – 12 ounces
Sea salt and black pepper – to taste

Instructions:
- Cook the chopped bacon in a twelve-inch cast iron skillet over medium-low heat until it is crispy. You want to cook it over low heat and no higher so that you are able to render more of its fat.

- Remove the bacon from the skillet and set it aside. You should have about one-eighth of an inch of fat remaining in the skillet. If you don't you can compensate by adding in another fat of your choice such as lard, ghee, or coconut oil.

- While you continue to cook on the stove preheat the oven to four hundred degrees Fahrenheit.

- Increase the heat of the cast iron skillet to medium-high and add the sweet potatoes to the hot bacon fat. Allow the sweet potatoes to cook without stirring, until the bottom of them turns golden-brown. After the bottom of the cubes are golden, stir them around and continue to cook until they just begin to soften.

- Increase the heat of the skillet to high and add in the bell pepper, onion, and zucchini. Allow the vegetables to cook until they just begin to soften.

- Remove the skillet from the heat and stir in the cooked bacon.

- With a spoon create six wells in the cooked vegetable mixture, and then crack an egg into each well.

- Place the skillet in the oven and allow it to cook for nine to fifteen minutes until the eggs are fully set.

Instant Pot Breakfast Casserole

This casserole is made easy and quick by being cooked in the Instant Pot, or another electric pressure cooker of your choice. The eggs are perfectly complimented with delicious grass-fed breakfast sausage, bright kale, and sweet potato.

Ingredients:
Water – 1.5 cups
Large eggs, beaten – 8
Leeks, sliced – 1.33 cups
Garlic, minced – 2 cloves
Coconut oil – 2 tablespoons
Sweet potato, peeled and grated – .66 cup
Kale, chopped – 1.5 cups
Grass-fed breakfast sausage, cooked – 1.5 cups
Sea salt – 1 teaspoon

Instructions:

- Set the Instant Pot to the sauté setting and melt the coconut oil before adding in the sliced leeks, minced garlic, and chopped kale. Allow them to sauté until softened.

- Remove the vegetables from the instant pot and place into a large bowl. Add in the beaten eggs, shredded sweet potato, and cooked breakfast sausage.

- Add the water and a trivet into the pressure cooker.

- Grease an oven proof pan or bowl that can fit into your pressure cooker, pour the egg and vegetable mixture into it, and then carefully set it onto the trivet that is in the Instant Pot.

- Lock the Instant Pot Lid and set the steam nozzle to cook so that the steam doesn't escape.

- Cook the casserole for twenty-five minutes on high-pressure and then quick release it. To quick release, you turn the steam nozzle to allow all of the steam to escape the pot immediately after the timer announces that the cooking time is complete.

- Slice the casserole into six portions and enjoy!

Sweet Potato Bowl

This bowl is full of nutrients, but the best thing about it is the flavor! It is creamy, sweet, and topped with cinnamon and berries. My favorite is blueberries, but you can always replace it with your favorite. If you want to add in some extra protein, you can always serve it with a side of bacon or grass-fed breakfast sausage.

Ingredients:
Sweet potato, cooked – 1, large
Coconut milk – 3 tablespoons
Almond butter – 2 tablespoons
Blueberries - .25 cup
Cinnamon – a couple dashes
Full-fat coconut milk – optional, for topping

Instructions:
- In a blender combine the cooked sweet potato, coconut milk, and almond butter until it is completely smooth.

- Pour it into a bowl and top with blueberries, cinnamon, and the extra full-fat coconut milk, if you desire.

- If you don't have fresh blueberries, you can always warm up some frozen blueberries.

Grain-Free Veggie Wraps

Wraps are awesome because you can eat them with your hands like a sandwich. It makes them wonderful to eat on-the-go. They are also full of vegetables, which turns them green. It's as simple as blending the ingredients together and quickly cooking them in a skillet before filling them with your favorite ingredients.

Ingredients:
Large eggs – 3
Large handful of kale, parsley, or other dark leafy greens
Fresh herbs, such as basil, tarragon, or thyme – 1 teaspoon
Arrowroot powder – 2 tablespoons
Sea salt – .33 teaspoon
Coconut oil

Instructions:
- Add the eggs, greens, herbs, arrowroot powder, and sea salt into a blender. Allow it to blend completely until it is liquefied.

- Over medium-low heat, place an eight-inch skillet and allow it to preheat. Allow the skillet to heat until water when dropped on it sizzles and evaporates. Brush the skillet with coconut oil before cooking each of the wraps, in order to prevent sticking.

- Measure out the batter for each wrap with a one-quarter cup measuring scoop. If the first wrap doesn't turn out perfectly that's okay. Just like when cooking pancakes, the first wrap is a test. After the first wrap, you may need to either increase the heat or lower it.

- When pouring the batter into the skillet hold the handle and slightly turn the wrist so that you can turn the pan in a circular motion, this will allow the batter to spread out into a circular disk.

- Closely watch the batter while it cooks. Once the batter begins to look firm and dry, then it is ready to flip it with a spatula. To do this you need to first lift the edges of the circle with the spatula. Once it fully lives in the center, you can flip it without it breaking.

- While it needs to be dry enough to flip, try not to overcook it. If it becomes too dry then it will become brittle and might break while filling with ingredients later on.

- Repeat the process until all of the wraps are cooked.

- Fill the wraps with your favorite ingredients. You could make it hamburger flavored, taco, BLT, chicken salad, or any other Paleo-friendly options.

Sweet Potato Nachos

Just because you are on the Paleolithic lifestyle doesn't mean you are unable to enjoy some of your favorite Tex-Mex or Game Day foods. Top these homemade sweet potato chips with your favorite guacamole, fresh salsa, and beef or chicken and you are all set for a good time!

Ingredients:
Sweet potatoes, peeled – 2
Black ground pepper - .25 teaspoon
Avocado oil – 1 tablespoon
Sea salt - .5 teaspoon
Guacamole – .25 cup
Salsa - .25 cup
Cooked beef or chicken, shredded – 1 pounding
jalapeños, thinly sliced – 1
Scallions, sliced – 3

Instructions:
- Thinly slice the sweet potatoes using a mandolin and then place them on a baking sheet lined with parchment paper.
- Toss the sweet potato slices with avocado oil, sea salt, and black pepper and place them in an oven preheated at 375 deg. F.
- Once the chips are crispy remove them from the oven and allow them to cool.
- Top the cooked sweet potato chips with guacamole, salsa, shredded meat, jalapeños, and scallions. You can add any other favorite Paleo-friendly toppings, as well.

Chipotle Chicken Salad

Chicken salad is a great option on the Paleo diet, for any meal or snack. You can either eat it on its own, on top of a bed or greens, which sliced apples, homemade sweet potato chips, or many other ingredients. You can keep the chicken cooked in the fridge or freezer to easily use at any time. To cook the chicken, you can either roast it or cook it whole in the Instant Pot.

Ingredients:
Chicken, cooked and diced – 1 pound
Onion, finely diced - .5 cup
Celery, finely chopped – 4 stalks
Avocado oil - .66 cup
Large egg – 1
Cayenne pepper - .25 teaspoon
Lemon juice – 1 teaspoon
Garlic powder - .25 teaspoon
Chipotle adobo sauce – 1 teaspoon
Sea salt and ground black pepper – to taste

Instructions:
- In a bowl combine the chopped chicken, diced onion, and finely diced celery.
- Place the avocado oil, egg, cayenne pepper, lemon juice, garlic powder, chipotle adobo sauce, sea salt, and black pepper in a container. Using an immersion blender blend until the mayonnaise thickens to the preferred consistency. You want it to reach a similar consistency as store-bought mayo. This should take an average of thirty seconds.
- Add the mayonnaise to the chicken mixture and combine it.

Chicken Nuggets

When you need an easy protein filled meal for the road, mid-afternoon snack, or something that you can get the kids to eat, these chicken nuggets are the solution. Using Paleo mayonnaise is the perfect breading, and you can even dip them in mayonnaise when eating!

Ingredients:
Large boneless chicken thighs – 2
Paleo mayonnaise - .25 cup
Almond flour – 1 cup
Apple cider vinegar – 1 teaspoon
Black pepper - .25 teaspoons
Garlic powder - .5 teaspoon
Avocado oil – 2 tablespoons
Sea salt - .5 teaspoon
Onion powder - .5 teaspoon

Instructions:
- Chop the chicken thighs into one-inch cubes and toss them with the sea salt, onion powder, black pepper, and garlic powder.
- In a small bowl combine the apple cider vinegar with the Paleo-friendly mayonnaise.
- In another bowl place the almond flour.
- Coat the chicken pieces with the mayonnaise and then in the flour.
- To cook the nuggets place them in a large skillet over medium-high heat with coconut oil. Place them in a single layer so that they aren't touching each other. Each side of the nugget will need to cook for about three minutes, then flip them and allow the other side to cook.

Instant Pot Chili

Just because you can't have beans doesn't mean you are unable to enjoy a warm pot of chili. While some chili might have to cook for hours on the stove, this pot can cook for only thirty-minutes! Despite the shorter cooking time, it still packs all of the flavor. This is because when cooking under pressure food naturally develops more depth of flavor quicker than it otherwise would.

Instructions:
Ground beef, choose one with a high fat content – 2 pounds
Beef broth - .66 cup
Sea salt – 1 teaspoon
Large onion, diced – 1
Cumin – 1 tablespoon
Black pepper, ground - .5 teaspoon
Tomato paste - .25 cup
Garlic powder – 1 tablespoon
Chili powder – 3 tablespoons
Fire-roasted tomatoes, with the liquid – 28-ounce can

Instructions:
- Set the Instant pot to the sauté setting and add in the ground beef and diced onions. If the beef isn't high enough fat content and begins to stick, then you can add in some oil. Allow them to cook together until the meat is browned, about five to seven minutes.

- Using a wooden or plastic spatula break up the ground beef as it browns, and then add in the tomato paste, cumin, chili powder, and garlic powder. Allow all of the ingredients to cook together for two additional minutes.

- Add the beef broth and the canned fire-roasted tomatoes to the Instant pot and combine.

- Lock the lid of the pressure cooker and set the spout to seal to prevent the steam from escaping. Put the Instant Pot on the bean/chili option and allow it to cook under high-pressure for thirty minutes.

- Quick release the steam from the Instant Pot and serve as-is or with your favorite Paleo-friendly chili options, such as avocado.

Instant Pot Tomato Soup

There is nothing like a comforting bowl of tomato soup. You may not think you can have the perfect tomato soup without cream and Paleo-friendly, but you absolutely can! That is because when made in the Instant Pot and with these ingredients it is creamy while still being vibrant and bright. The herbs are aromatic and comforting, pairing perfectly with the tomatoes.

Ingredients:
Onion, diced - .5 cup
Tomato paste – 1 tablespoon
Garlic, minced – 4 cloves
Carrots, chopped – 2
Avocado oil – 1 tablespoon
Full-fat coconut milk – 14 ounces
Coconut Aminos – 2 tablespoons
Chicken broth – 2 cups
San Marzano canned tomatoes, chopped – 28 ounces
Bay leaf – 1
Dried thyme - .5 teaspoon
Fresh basil, chopped - .25 cup
Sea salt and black pepper – to taste

Instructions:
- Set the Instant Pot to sauté and cook together the onion, carrots, garlic, and avocado oil until both the onions and carrots are soft, about five to ten minutes.
- Add the tomato paste to the pot and cook it while stirring for a couple minutes, until the paste begins to caramelize.
- Add in the chopped canned tomatoes, bay leaf, thyme, Coconut Aminos, and chicken broth.
- Set the Instant Pot to manual and allow it to cook on high-pressure for fifteen minutes.
- When the time is complete set it to quick release.
- Once finished cooking, add in the coconut milk and sea salt, stirring until it's fully combined.

- In batches slowing puree all of the tomato soup in a blender until it's smooth.
- Serve the soup with chopped basil and black pepper.

Chapter 6: Sometimes You May Want to Indulge

Sometimes you may want something to drink other than plain water, feel the craving for chocolate, or you may be wondering if you can still have your morning cup of coffee. In this chapter, your questions about indulging on the Paleo diet will be answered!

We all know that water is Paleo. In fact, it is highly recommended to drink large quantities of filtered pure drinking water to stay hydrated. You want to listen to your body and drink when you are thirsty. But don't use this as an excuse to drink too little water. If you wait to drink until you feel thirsty then you might be dehydrated. You may also be thirsty when you are simply hungry, so if you feel hungry when you've eaten well, then try drinking more water and see if that helps.

The general recommendation is to make sure that you are drinking a minimum of half of your body's weight in pounds in ounces of water. This means that if you weight one-hundred and fifty pounds that you should drink seventy-five ounces of water.

If you want to increase this even more, just be aware to never drink more than one liter of water within the span of an hour. This is because your liver is physically unable to process more water than this in such a short period of time. It can cause quite a bit of damage to your body and liver and is rather dangerous. Thankfully, this is not a concern for most people.

If you don't feel like plain water some other options include sparkling water. But always be careful to check the ingredients for non-Paleo ingredients. For instance, Tonic usually has sugar added to it, making it not an option on the Paleo diet.

You want brands that only have one or two ingredients that are Paleo-friendly, such as carbonated water and "natural flavor." One of these brands that is a favorite is LaCroix.

As you can see, contrary to popular belief, you can enjoy more drinks other than water while on the Paleo diet.

Paleo Drinks:
- Filtered water
- Sparkling water
- Mineral water
- Kombucha
- Caffeine-free herbal tea

Only in Moderation:
- Alcohol
- Coffee
- Black tea, green tea, or other teas with caffeine
- Coconut water, but be careful due to the high-carbohydrate level
- Drinks sweetened with stevia or sugar alcohols such as erythritol
- Vegetable and fruit juice when freshly-juiced and it contains the pulp
- Drinks with natural sweeteners such as honey, coconut sap, and maple

Drinks to Avoid:
- Beer and other drinks with gluten

- Fruit juice
- Dairy-based kefir
- Energy drinks
- Sodas
- Sports drinks
- Anything with artificial sweeteners, dyes, preservatives, or flavors

More About Alcohol

Many people are shocked that you can have alcohol on the Paleo diet, but it's true! That is, as long as you only drink it in moderation.

Certain alcohol has been proven to have benefits such as reducing the risk of developing gallstones, heart disease, and type II diabetes. Although, it is important to remember that alcohol can also have the opposite effect if you drink it in excess or overly frequently.

There are three types of alcohol, this includes wine, beer, and spirits. Wine and beer are made by fermenting sugar and starch that is naturally found in plants. This includes grapes, rice, and coconut for wine. Beer is usually made from wheat or barley.

While spirits are also made with grains, they are then distilled in order to greatly increase the amount of alcohol they consume. This process has been shown to remove gluten and other proteins that are found within grains. Although, some brands might later add gluten back into the distilled alcohol with the addition of dyes or other alcohols.

Spirits:

This category includes vodka, whiskey, rum, and tequila. Thankfully, these spirits are usually Paleo-friendly, in moderation, as long as they are in their pure forms without sugars, dyes, or other alcohols added. But you need to be careful when drinking these because they have a significant amount of alcohol.

The best choices for spirits are those that are made without grains or at least are certified as gluten-free. The spirits that are lighter in color and clear are better choices than the spirits that are darker in color. This is because the darker colors contain more sugar. Some favorites include silver agave tequila and potato-based vodka. A certified gluten-free brand is Tito's, especially for those on the Paleo lifestyle who love to party.

Be careful of cocktails, as they are almost always full of sugar or other sweeteners. Instead, you can mix your spirits with sparkling water, soda water, seltzer, or even LaCroix. Add a splash of lemon or lime juice to finish it off.

One favorite which is easy to get your hands on is a simple vodka with a twist of lime or a martini. If you really want a cocktail, you can ask a bartender to omit the sweeteners. Not only does avoiding the sugar improve your health and weight, but it will also lessen any hangover you might have!

Wine:

One of the best options on the Paleolithic lifestyle is wine. Firstly, wine is lower in alcohol. This means that you are less likely to drink too much and experience negative side effects. Secondly, wine is full of important antioxidants, including resveratrol. This is an extremely helpful and anti-cancer antioxidant that is mostly found in the skin of grapes, and therefore wine. Try to find a wine that is organic and sulfite-free.

You may also choose hard apple cider, port wine, and mead which is a type of wine made by the fermentation of honey.

Just remember the golden rule of drinking when Paleo: Pay attention to your body. If you find that your body doesn't respond well to something, then don't drink it.

Beer:

Since beer is generally full of wheat and therefore gluten, it should be completely avoided. Even gluten-free beer should be avoided due to its grain content, which may cause increased weight, inflammation, leaky gut, and autoimmune disease.

The All-Important Coffee

Studies show that coffee contains many benefits. These include increased alertness, mood, memory, fat burning, improved athletic performance, and reduced risk of Parkinson's, Alzheimer's disease, and cancer.

Although, it is important to remember that these benefits are only when we drink coffee in moderate amounts. This means you shouldn't drink more than two cups of coffee a day, and those two cups should be earlier in the day so as to not disrupt your sleep.

Many people use coffee as a way to get through the day. But by relying on coffee people can develop adrenal fatigue as well as unstable blood sugar. If you are pregnant or have an autoimmune disease, type II diabetes, adrenal fatigue, a slow metabolism, uncontrolled hypertension, or large amounts of stress, then you might want to avoid all caffeine.

Every now and then you may want to go on a caffeine cleanse and avoid all traces of it. This will enable that you don't become dependent on it.

If you aren't a coffee person but you enjoy tea, then you can enjoy your tea as others would their coffee. Keep it in moderation and try not to become dependent. Out of the various teas, it is best to choose green tea. This is because green tea is high in antioxidants and has even been shown to promote weight loss.

Chocolate to the Rescue

Chocolate is amazing, and there are very few people who are willing to give it up. In fact, whether or not chocolate is Paleo is one of the most common questions regarding the Paleo lifestyle. For those of you wondering, while our Paleolithic ancestors didn't eat chocolate, it is permitted with moderation. This is because, despite not being eaten during the Paleo period, dark chocolate has many health benefits.

The best choice for chocolate is to make your own. You can do this by combining together cocoa, honey, and either coconut oil or cocoa butter. Afterward, simply pour it into molds and chill it until set. It will need to be stored in the fridge to prevent melting.

When buying dark chocolate keep it to eighty-five percent dark or higher, nothing lighter than this as it will have too much sweetener.

One popular brand is Theo, who has an eighty-five percent dark chocolate. Their chocolate is organic and fair trade. It also does not include preservatives, soy lecithin, or any other non-Paleo ingredients aside from sugar. The only ingredients found in this chocolate is cocoa beans, sugar, and vanilla.

But be sure to only eat a small amount at a time, especially due to the sugar!

What About Dairy and Red Meat?

Paleo is damaging to the gut and seventy-five percent of the world's population is intolerant or allergic. All dairy is prohibited. Although you can have ghee, as the dairy has been removed from the fat in the butter.

You've most likely heard a thousand times that it's not good to eat too much red meat. While this is certainly true for feedlot beef that is fed corn and other grains, grass-fed beef is different. In fact, grass-fed beef is extremely high in omega three fatty acids, vitamin E, vitamin K, beta-carotene, and antioxidants. All of these nutrients are found in a much higher degree in grass-fed beef than corn-fed beef.

You don't have to worry about red meat too much, as long as you are eating it in balance. This means making sure that you are enjoying other sources of non-red meat, as well, such as turkey, chicken, and fish.

Conclusion

During the Paleolithic era, people ate what was naturally available to them, exercised through their day simply by living actively, and this promoted their health. Studies now show that eating in the same way as our ancestors can promote our health, as well. You have to look no further than the story of Nell Stephenson in chapter one. Just as she was able to take her health into her own hands and once again passionately live her life, so too can you.

The Paleo diet may be quite different from what you are used to, especially if you are living on the Standard American Diet. But that doesn't mean it has to be difficult. You can simply enjoy a diet rich with a variety of vegetables, fruits, tubers, meats, fish and shellfish, nuts, seeds, and healthy fats. You can even enjoy a glass of wine, a martini, or a cup of coffee on occasion!

Don't let fear hold you back from the life you deserve. You too can enjoy a full life.

Thank you.

www.ingramcontent.com/pod-product-compliance
Lightning Source LLC
Chambersburg PA
CBHW021128080526
44587CB00012B/1183